Public Policy and the Black Hospital

Recent Titles in
Contributions in Afro-American and African Studies

Public Policy and the Black Hospital

From Slavery to Segregation to Integration

Mitchell F. Rice
and Woodrow Jones, Jr.

Contributions in Afro-American and African Studies,
Number 165

Greenwood Press
Westport, Connecticut • London

Library of Congress Cataloging-in-Publication Data

Rice, Mitchell F.
   Public policy and the black hospital : from slavery to segregation
to integration / Mitchell F. Rice and Woodrow Jones, Jr.
      p.   cm.—(Contributions in Afro-American and African
studies, ISSN 0069-9624 ; no. 165)
   Includes bibliographical references and index.
   ISBN 0-313-26309-4 (alk. paper)
   1. Afro-Americans—Hospitals—History. I. Jones, Woodrow.
II. Title. III. Series.
RA981.A45R53 1994
362.1'1'08996073—dc20   93-4851

British Library Cataloguing in Publication Data is available.

Library of Congress Catalog Card Number: 93-4851
ISBN: 0-313-26309-4
ISSN: 0069-9624

First published in 1994

Greenwood Press, 88 Post Road West, Westport, CT 06881
An imprint of Greenwood Publishing Group, Inc.

Printed in the United States of America

The paper used in this book complies with the
Permanent Paper Standard issued by the National
Information Standards Organization (Z39.48-1984).

10 9 8 7 6 5 4 3 2 1

TO THE SURVIVAL OF
THE BLACK HOSPITAL

Contents

Tables

Introduction

Edward H. Beardsley in *A History of Neglect: Health Care for Blacks and Mill Workers in the Twentieth-Century South* (1987) remarked that, in the area of Black health history, "The list of key secondary works is admittedly short, but that is merely a sign of how much remains to be done in the area of Black health history."[1] This book adds to a small but growing body of literature in one area of Black health history--the rise of hospital care and hospital services provided to Blacks from the antebellum era to the integration era, a period of some 150 years. The book's primary aim is threefold: (1) to document the history, development, and significance of Black hospitals and point out their special place in Black health history; (2) to document Black hospitals' sources of funding, support, and development; and (3) to explore why so few Black hospitals remain as we approach the twenty-first century.

Specifically, the book examines and explores the Black hospital from a public policy perspective. Two historical public policies that are the major subjects of discussion are the federal Freedmen's Bureau policy from 1865 to 1869 and the federal Hill-Burton Act from 1946 to 1974. The former policy, while providing hospital care to former slaves, maintained the policy and custom of separate hospital facilities in cities and towns, especially in the South. The latter policy, about eight decades later, provided little change in discriminatory or exclusionary practices and policies in hospital services for Blacks. Further, the year 1965 was the beginning of the hospital integration era. Yet, it was after this time that Black hospitals began to decrease dramatically in number. This book examines the impact of the integration era on the decline of the Black hospital. In particular, the impact of two contemporary federal public health policies, Medicare and Medicaid, are discussed in the context of the decline of Black hospitals.

Black hospitals are defined as hospitals founded by Black and/or White individuals, organizations, and interests for the purpose of providing hospital care primarily or exclusively to Blacks.[2] Mitchell F. Rice observes that "despite their longevity and historically significant role in serving the health care needs of the Black community, especially during the segregation era, the existence of hospitals which primarily or exclusively served Blacks is unknown to most individuals and [much of the medical field] in both Black and White communities."[3] Black hospitals or hospitals that serve a largely Black constituency have been classified into three broad types: "segregated, [B]lack-controlled, and demographically determined."[4] Segregated Black hospitals were those established by Whites to serve Blacks. These facilities existed primarily in the South. Black-controlled institutions are those founded by Blacks to train and to provide clinical and educational opportunities for Black physicians and nurses. Segregated and Black-controlled hospitals represent the historical Black hospital. These hospitals were established because of segregation and discriminatory policies and practices. Demographically determined Black hospitals are those institutions that progressively evolved into Black hospitals. This situation was brought on by area or neighborhood demographic changes, that is, a locale's changing from a largely White population to a largely Black one.[5] These hospitals may be referred to as transitional Black hospitals.

The existing literature on Black hospital care and Black hospitals is scattered and, for the most part, located in specialty journals and publications, lesser-known publications, or a part of larger studies on Black American history. Journals and publications such as the *Journal of the National Medical Association*, *The Crisis*, *The Southern Workman*, and *Opportunity* provided extensive reports on Black hospital development from the 1900s to 1960s. However, since Beardsley's 1987 volume a few works have been written, particularly by Black researchers, that provide rich and fascinating accounts of various aspects of the role of Black hospitals in Black health care. Vanessa Northington Gamble's *The Black Community Hospital* (1989) "is an overview of the [B]lack community hospitals," and Gamble gives only cursory attention to public policy and political forces that help to shape and define the Black community hospital.[6]

Nevertheless, the work represents the most recent comprehensive account of the Black community hospital. David McBride's *Integrating the City of Medicine: Blacks in Philadelphia Health Care, 1910-1965* (1989) is a more in-depth study, that "traces the structural development and the social and political experiences of one urban community of [B]lack medical professionals as America passed through 'separate but equal' segregation to the post-*Brown* period of legally enforced integration."[7]   As a part of the study, McBride provides a historical account of Black hospital development in Philadelphia.

Unlike these works, this book presents a more comprehensive and in-depth examination of Black hospital development within a public policy and philanthropy context.   Within this context, the importance of the role and significance of Black hospitals can be better understood in American society in general and in the Black community in particular.

Even the major literature that focuses on the historical development of both public and private hospitals in the United States scarcely touches hospital services and hospital care provided to Blacks. A most recent and complete account of hospital development in the United States, Charles Rosenberg's *The Care of Strangers: The Rise of America's Hospital System* (1987) does not discuss Black hospital development nor hospital care for Blacks. Rosenberg's discussion of the early history of Massachusetts General Hospital does not mention that a Black was admitted by error in 1829 or that a Black was specifically denied admission to the hospital in 1836.[8]   H. F. Dowling's *City Hospitals: The Undercare of the Underprivileged* (1982) provides no account of Black hospital development or of Black hospitals in the inner city.[9] Prominent social and medical historians and medical humanists have, with few exceptions, ignored the Black hospital as an important subject of inquiry and discussion. Even the major works on Blacks in medicine and health care, such as Herbert M. Morais's *The History of the Negro in Medicine* (1967), do not provide comprehensive historical accounts of hospital care available to Blacks especially in the late nineteenth and early twentieth centuries.[10]

From before the Civil War period to the 1960s, Black hospitals owned and operated by Black and White community interests provided a significant amount of health care to Black Americans. The first Black hospitals in the United States were dedicated to providing care to Blacks whose access to White hospitals was severely restricted, if not nonexistent, because of segregation policies. Prior to the Civil War, hospital care was virtually nonexistent for Blacks. Only a few hospital facilities provided care to Blacks. The first American hospital, built on Manhattan Island in 1658 for sick soldiers, did provide care to West Indian Company Blacks, and the Colored Orphan Asylum established in New York City in 1836 did provide care to some Blacks.[11] The Georgia Infirmary, which was chartered by the Georgia General Assembly to open in Savannah on December 24, 1832, was the first hospital facility established by Whites to provide hospital care to Blacks.[12] In 1852, a second facility (an infirmary) was opened by Whites in Savannah for Black cases requiring "medical and surgical treatment,", except contagious disease cases.[13]

The first hospital system for Blacks in the United States was founded in the public sector. This hospital system was created as a result of federal policy. These hospitals were operated by the Bureau of Freedmen, Refugees, and Abandoned Lands.[14] Freedmen's Hospital in Washington, D.C. (now Howard University Hospital), began operating in 1863. The federal government sponsored the hospital in an attempt to deal with a number of diseases that were widespread among the Black population in the District of Columbia.[15] A Black physician, Major Alexander T. Augusta, was placed in charge during the first year. He was also the first Black physician to head a hospital in the U.S.[16] The hospital had a mixed staff and admitted patients of any color. William Montague Cobb states that Freedmen's Hospital was "the most important single hospital contributing to the medical development of the Negro."[17] By the turn of the twentieth century more than 150 Black hospitals had come into existence.[18]

From 1891 to the 1960s Black hospitals or those serving a largely Black constituency were founded in major cities throughout the West, East, South, and Midwest such as Chicago, New Orleans, Miami, Washington, Detroit, Atlanta, Baltimore, Dallas, Kansas City (Missouri), St. Louis, and New York. Some smaller cities having Black hospitals during this time span were Flint, Michigan; Nashville, Tennessee; Roanoke, Virginia; Evanston, Illinois; Selma, Alabama; Montgomery, Alabama; Tuskegee, Alabama; Greensboro, North Carolina; and Richmond, Virginia. This book brings together under one cover and as a single source the hospital care saga in the Black community.

This book is divided into five chapters. The first chapter provides an overview of slave hospital care and points out that slave health was important to slave owners because of economic reasons. Chapter One also describes slave hospitals on Southern plantations and points out the extent to which the federal Freedmen's Bureau provided hospital and medical care to the freed slaves. The Freedmen's Bureau was the federal government's first policy initiative to assist freed slaves in several social areas, including health. Chapter Two discusses in considerable detail what is known as "The Black Hospital Movement." This was the period after 1900 and particularly in the 1920s and 1930s in which the number of Black hospitals dramatically increased. Of particular note in Chapter Two is the role of the National Hospital Association (a Black organization), Black self-help, and private philanthropy in the growth and increase of Black hospitals.

Chapter Three provides brief descriptions of fifty-seven Black hospitals. These hospitals range from simple, small structures to ones with several rooms and some equipment to ones with a large number of rooms, modern equipment and facilities, specialty rooms, and specialty services. Chapter Four gives attention to the Hill-Burton Act of 1946 and its impact on Black hospital development and on the maintenance of hospital segregation. The Hill-Burton Act was the federal government's attempt to construct and modernize hospitals throughout the United States. This chapter also examines the legal and political forces that led to the formal integration of hospitals in both patients and physicians. Of special interest here is the lawsuit affecting the Hill-Burton Act and hearings by the United States Commission on Civil Rights. Chapter Five explores the forces that have led to the virtual demise of Black hospitals. By early 1992 only six traditionally Black hospitals remained in operation and service. The chapter discusses the role of two contemporary federal policies, Medicaid and Medicare, on the decline of Black hospitals.

This book has been in progress for several years and would not have been possible without the support of several organizations and individuals. Among these are the Rockefeller Archive Center and the U.S. National Endowment for the Humanities for financial support for archival research. A special thanks goes to Shirley DeJean, whose high-quality word processing skills led to the final production of this volume. For any errors of omission or commission, the authors takes full responsibility.

NOTES

1. Edward H. Beardsley, *A History of Neglect: Health Care for Blacks and Mill Workers in the Twentieth Century South* (Knoxville, TN: University of Tennessee Press, 1987), p. 369.

2. This definition focuses on historically Black hospitals and those hospitals that transformed into hospitals serving a largely Black clientele. Classifying hospitals by race today raises some serious issues and concerns. See Nathaniel Wesley and Julie Benton Link, "Institutional Survival: Barriers to the Survival of Black and Other Health Care Facilities and Institutions Serving Predominantly Black Populations" (Paper presented at the Harlem Hospital Centennial National Health Conference, New York City, April 1988).

3. Mitchell F. Rice, "Black Hospitals: Institutional Impacts on Black Families." In Harold E. Cheatham and James B. Stewart (eds.), *Black Families: Interdisciplinary Perspectives* (New Brunswick, NJ: Transaction Publishers, 1990), p. 50.

4. Vanessa Northington Gamble, *The Black Community Hospital* (New York: Garland Publishing Co., 1969), p. 2.

5. Ibid., pp. 3-4.

6. Ibid., p. 2.

7. David McBride, *Integrating the City of Medicine: Blacks in Philadelphia Health Care, 1910-1965* (Philadelphia: Temple University Press, 1989), pp. xv-xvi.

8. Charles E. Rosenberg, *The Care of Strangers: The Rise of America's Hospital System* (New York: Basic Books, 1987). See also Charles E. Rosenberg, "Inward Vision and Outward Glance: The Shaping of the American Hospital, 1880-1914." *Bulletin of the History of Medicine* 53 (1979): 346-391.

9. H. F. Dowling, *City Hospitals: The Undercare of the Underprivileged* (Cambridge, MA: Harvard University Press, 1982).

10. Herbert M. Morais, *The History of the Negro in Medicine* (NY: Publishers Co., 1967).

11. See "Bed of Procrustes" (Chapter 4). *Journal of the National Medical Association (Supplement)* 73 (1981): 1219-1220.

12. H. Hewes, "Georgia Infirmary: First Hospital in the United States Founded for Negroes." *Negro History Bulletin* (October 1945): 2-23.

13. "Infirmary for Negroes at Savannah, Geo." *Charleston Medical Journal and Review* 7 (1852): 724.

14. See T. Holt, C. Smith-Parker, and R. Terborg-Penn, *A Special Mission: The Story of Freedmen's Hospital* (Washington, D.C.: Division of Academic Affairs, Howard University, 1975) and Herbert M. Morais, *The History of the Negro in Medicine*, pp. 42-44.

15. Holt, Smith-Parker, and Terborg-Penn, *A Special Mission*, pp. 11-13.

16. William M. Cobb, "Integration in Medicine: A National Need." *Journal of the National Medical Association* 49 (January 1957): 1-7.

17. Ibid., p. 2.

18. Emily Friedman, "Private Black Hospitals: A Long Tradition Facing Change." *Hospitals* (July 1, 1978): 63-68.

Public Policy
and the
Black Hospital

1

Black Hospital Care from the Plantation Era through Post-Reconstruction

During the plantation period slaves were most important to owners. In some instances, sickly and diseased slaves were purchased by physicians at low prices, restored to health, and sold to plantation owners at an enormous profit.[1] As slaves represented the greatest and most important part of a plantation owner's property, it was critical that slaves be cared for. In 1860 an estimated total of four million slaves were valued at $2 billion.[2] For economic reasons, the health maintenance of slaves was an important and necessary activity. Richard H. Shryock, a noted scholar of the history of medicine, observed that "the slaves was perhaps the only group of poor workers in whose health their employers had a direct property interest, and for whom they felt a direct responsibility; and for these reasons they sometimes received more care than did Southern "poor Whites" or Northern laborers."[3]

SLAVE PLANTATION HOSPITALS

Plantation owners and overseers were told repeatedly that slave health should receive special attention. The *Cotton Plantation Record and Account Book* advised, "The health of the negroes under your charge is an important matter. Much of the usual sickness among them is the result of carelessness and mismanagement . . . Whenever, you find that the case is one you do not understand, send for a physician."[4] The *Rules on a Rice Estate* and *Plantation Rules* offered similar advice on slave health management.[5] *Planter's and Mariner's Medical Companion*, first published in 1807, became widely accepted as the family doctor book among plantation masters and overseers.[6]

The health of pregnant and lying-in women and of infants and children was of particular concern, since they represented the future of the plantation.[7]

On many large plantations, medical care included the establishment of plantation hospitals and infirmaries, or "sick houses" as slaves referred to them. Mary Louise Marshall noted that "All plantations of any size maintained well-ordered hospitals and all negroes who were sick were required to remain here until able to return to work."[8] In many cases an older Black woman was placed in charge of slaves and received advice from the overseer, owner or doctor. In fact, some Black medical providers and attendants were considered so knowledgeable that Whites consulted with them on the treatment of various Black illnesses and ailments.[9] In some instances, their expertise became the envy of White physicians. These White physicians sought legal means to prevent Blacks from rendering medical care. For example, a Tennessee court ruled that slaves could not practice medical care.[10]

Martha Carolyn Mitchell observed that "practically every plantation had a hospital of some kind ranging from a rather well equipped establishment to a few bare beds in an empty room."[11] Todd L. Savitt documented the existence of slave plantation hospitals in Richmond, Prince George, and Fairfax Counties in Virginia.[12] White physicians, usually in their beginning years of practice, would contract with plantations to provide health care.[13] V. A. Moody pointed out that, on large sugar plantations in Louisiana, "In order to have slaves properly attended it was necessary to have a well-ordered hospital as a part of its equipment."[14] According to Moody, one such hospital located on "Valcour Aime's [Louisiana] Plantation about 1853 was said to be 64 feet square and to contain seven rooms and an immense 'verandah.'"[15] Other hospitals were believed to have existed on the Magnolia, Bayou Cotonniere, and Houma sugar plantations.[16] C. S. Sydnor traced slave plantation hospitals in Mississippi to 1831.[17] William Postell identified several slave plantation hospitals in Mississippi and Louisiana and pointed out that the Magnolia Hill Plantation in Natchez, Mississippi, had a slave hospital that was made of brick and measured thirty-two by twenty-three feet divided into two rooms.[18]

In Louisiana, the hospital on the Allston estate contained six rooms, fireplaces, and a piazza. On the Melrose Plantation, the slave hospital measured eighty by thirty-two feet with four rooms. The

Magnolia Hill Plantation hospital was made of brick and measured thirty-five by eighteen feet divided into two rooms. The Parlange Plantation slave hospital was a two-story brick building with four large rooms on each floor. A slave hospital also existed on the Ossabaw Island Plantation, Southdown Plantation, Holley Plantation, Waterloo Plantation, East Hermitage Plantation, A. Franklin Pugh Plantation, Rosedew Plantation, Pleasant Hill Plantation, Birdfield Plantation, and Dirleton Plantation.[19]

In many instances, slave plantation hospitals, especially on large plantations, contained separate rooms for men and women and had a confinement ward known as the "lying-in room" in which contagious cases were sometimes separated. In many cases, there was also a clinic connected to many hospitals called the "pharmacy," doctor's room, nurse's room or "medicine room." The clinic most often contained equipment, instruments, and medicine. The Parlange Plantation hospital had at least 166 separate medicinal items. Many large plantations used slave women as nurses and other slaves as hands and maintained records of treatment and deaths.[20]

R. W. Fogel and S. E. Engerman observed that one plantation with 168 slaves had a hospital consisting of a two story brick building that had eight large rooms and separate rooms for men and women.[21] One or more of the rooms were used as an outpatient clinic and a pharmacy. On smaller plantations, the hospital was merely an ordinary cabin reserved for the sick. In some instances masters set aside several rooms in their own houses for use as a hospital. According to Fogel and Engerman, the rationale for hospitalizing slaves was twofold: "It permitted the sick to receive special care including not only rest and medication but also special diets; it also isolated the sick slaves from the healthy ones and thus minimized the danger of contagion."[22]

In addition to plantation hospitals for the care of slaves, hospitals were organized and maintained by physicians or groups of physicians in large and small Southern cities and towns. Such hospitals existed in New Orleans, Savannah, Montgomery, Natchez, and Springfield, Louisiana. In Montgomery, Alabama, a small two-story slave hospital was maintained in the rear of the home of Dr. J. Marion Sims.[23] The hospital consisted of sixteen beds, twelve for patients and four for servants. In Savannah, Georgia an infirmary for slaves was advertised as "being well equipped, having competent nurses, comfortable beds, well-ventilated wards, extensive pleasure grounds, and a good dietary department."[24]   In Natchez, Mississippi, an exclusive hospital for slaves, a two-story brick house sixty by twenty-four feet, was located just opposite the slave mart.   This facility was known as the Mississippi State Hospital. The Homeopathic Infirmary for slaves, also in Natchez, provided care to slaves for $1 per day. At least two hospitals in New Orleans provided wards for slaves: Dr. Stone's Infirmary or Maison de Sante' and the Circus Street Hospital. In the rural city of Springfield, Louisiana, Dr. George Colmer maintained a hospital exclusively for slaves.   The facility was known as the Infirmary for Slaves.[25]

The plantation hospital and health care provided to slaves, while generally not the best, did by some accounts improve their health status relative to free Blacks.   Comparative studies of the time reported that slave mortality rates were two to three times lower than those of free Blacks.[26] Thus slave plantation hospital and health care could be viewed as a sort of health insurance system. That is, as long as slaves had value, they had health insurance.

FREEDMEN'S BUREAU POLICY AND BLACK HOSPITAL CARE

Why a Black Hospital Health Program?

After Emancipation, the migration of thousands of rural Blacks to the cities exposed many to epidemic diseases for the first time, leading to an enormous health crisis. The situation forced the federal government to become directly concerned with the health care of Blacks. The government began debating legislation spearheaded by Republicans to help sick and destitute freedmen.[27] By 1863 the health and welfare of freedmen became a national issue and intensified as Congressional debate ensued. On March 3, 1865, Congress enacted the first Freedmen's Bureau legislation, and the federal government became intentionally involved in programs concerning Black health.[28] A subsequent Freedmen's bill was enacted in early 1866, only to be vetoed by President Andrew Johnson and reintroduced and passed by Congress in mid-1866. The Bureau was reauthorized by Congress and received appropriations each year until its activities ended on January 1, 1869. The bureau was mandated to focus on specific problems faced by the former slaves including education, employment, and health.[29] In the 1865 legislation, Congress created and funded a

Medical Division within the Bureau. However, as the severity of the freedmen's health problems was not recognized, the funding, supplies, staff, and organization of the Medical Division were insufficient and ineffective.[30] After these problems were addressed, the Freedmen's Bureau became more effective in serving the health needs of freedmen.

The Medical Division consisted of a Washington, D.C., office managed by the Chief Medical Officer (who reported to the Commissioner of the Bureau), a surgeon-in-chief or chief medical officer for each district (roughly each state), and surgeons and doctors assigned to each locality.[31] The Chief Medical Officer in Washington supervised the medical work through Surgeons-in-Chief in each state. Decisions were made by the Chief Medical Officer regarding the installation and expansion of medical facilities. The state's Surgeons-in-Chief made recommendations to the Chief Medical Officer concerning programs and activities in their states and supervised local Bureau physicians. Physicians employed by the Bureau were required to file monthly statistical reports with their Surgeons-in-Chief. The Medical Division operated three types of health care systems: hospitals, dispensaries, and home visitation programs.

Hospitals, Dispensaries, and Home Visits

The Freedmen's Bureau established urban hospitals and rural dispensaries of varying qualities throughout the South for Blacks. The Bureau rarely built its own facilities, but instead made use of available buildings such as abandoned mansions. These hospitals accommodated from 20 to 500 patients. Most hospitals had a staff of eight to ten people with larger hospitals having larger professional and nonprofessional staffs. Most hospitals never had the recommended staffing of one staff person per every ten patients, as prescribed by the Bureau *Officers Manual*.[32]

The dispensary was less expensive to operate and provided less-comprehensive service.[33] The dispensary was directed by a doctor, and a druggist provided free medicines.[34] The doctor maintained regular hours for outpatient care and made frequent home visits and referrals to Bureau hospitals.[35] Home visits provided a way for the Bureau to extend its health services to Blacks. House visits also provided a way to treat Blacks with less acute illnesses and diseases.[36]

These three types of systems allowed the Bureau to expand its health care system throughout much of the South.

The Freedmen's Bureau's Impact

During the four-year existence of the Freedmen's Bureau, more than ninety hospitals, dispensaries, and other kinds of health facilities were established throughout the South[37] in such cities as Chattanooga, Memphis, and Nashville, Tennessee; Louisville, Kentucky; Vicksburg and Lauderdale, Mississippi; Atlanta, Augusta, Columbus, Macon and Savannah, Georgia; Mobile, Alabama; New Orleans, Shreveport, Louisiana; Salisbury and Wilmington, North Carolina; and several locations in South Carolina. The Bureau employed as many as 118 physicians and 406 hospital attendants.[38] The Bureau provided virtually no care to freedmen in Texas and Florida and limited service in Kentucky and Tennessee.[39]

In Georgia in 1865 the Freedmen's Bureau established a medical department of five hospitals with a Surgeon-in-Chief, three medical officers, and seven private physicians under contract to administer the Bureau's public health work particularly among newly freed slaves.[40] Two Black physicians were appointed to work at the Georgia Bureau. C. H. Taylor, a Black assistant surgeon, was assigned to duty at the Lincoln Hospital in Savannah. Alexander T. Augusta, a Black physician educated in Canada who would become head of the Freedmen's Hospital in Washington, D.C., was placed in charge of Lincoln Hospital.[41] In addition, Bureau hospitals were established in Atlanta, Columbus, Macon, and Augusta.[42]

In South Carolina between the summer of 1865 and the close of 1868 the Medical Department of the Freedmen's Bureau had treated nearly 150,000 cases of illness among Blacks.[43] From mid-1865 to the end of 1868, the South Carolina Bureau treated about 150,000 Blacks and 20,000 Whites.[44] The Bureau in Mississippi consisted of a Surgeon-in-Chief, several army surgeons, private physicians, and attendants. The Mississippi Bureau is estimated to have treated 25,000.[45] In Kentucky, the Bureau established one hospital in Louisville, which operated from 1866 to 1868, and five dispensaries. A total of five physicians were employed in the Kentucky Bureau. At least 15,000 freedmen and other persons received care from the Kentucky Bureau.[46] In South Carolina, the Bureau staffed seventeen physicians and established five hospitals and several dispensaries.

Congress appropriated more than $2 million to the Medical Division of the Bureau during its existence. Yet, in some instances access to hospitals established by the Bureau was not always an advantage to sick freedmen. Sickness, disease, and even deaths were reported to have been caused by unsanitary conditions in hospitals at Lauderdale, Mississippi, and Macon, Georgia.[47] Further, inexperienced and unqualified doctors oftentimes were employed by the Bureau. Another problem was the lack of funds to buy proper food for patients, particularly fresh vegetables. Despite these problems C. M. Cooke observed that "In large measure, Blacks living at the time of the 1870 census owed their health to the free medical care provided by the Freedmen's Bureau."[48] While the Bureau fell far short of providing complete health care to millions of former slaves, it is estimated that the Bureau treated between 430,466 and 563,353 patients.[49]

Self-Help and Philanthropic Support to Freedmen

In addition to the Freedmen's Bureau, sanitary commissions and benevolent societies (formed by both Blacks and Whites) provided some health support to former slaves. These organizations expended "almost three million dollars in the South following the war."[50] Black societies such as the Nashville Colored Benevolent Society, which was organized in 1865 by twelve Nashville Blacks, were part of a self-help effort. The Society eventually expanded to twenty-seven branches throughout Tennessee. Sickness and burial benefits were important services that societies offered to Blacks. Other local Black societies and self-help groups formed after the Civil War included the Colored Ladies Relief Society, the Colored Home Mission Society, and the Nashville Provident Association. The Independent Order of Good Samaritans, the Daughters of Samaria, and the United Order of True Reformers were national organizations with branches in various locations throughout the South.[51]

Blacks also resorted to private means to establish small hospitals and infirmaries. Leonard Medical Hospital opened in 1885 in Raleigh, North Carolina, under the management of Shaw Institute, a local Black college. Free medicine was provided to Blacks at the hospital by the city. About the same time, the James Hale Infirmary was founded and financed by a prominent Black of the same name.[52]

From Exclusion to Segregation in Hospital Care

One problem that the Freedmen's Bureau did not solve was who would take responsibility for the freedmen's health after the Bureau discontinued its activities. Before the Civil War states and local governments had been spared the burden of caring for and supporting large numbers of ill and indigent Blacks. The plantation slave-welfare system had the responsibility. The relatively few free Blacks were left to care for themselves. After Emancipation and particularly during and after the Freedmen's Bureau, orphanages, hospitals, almshouses, and state facilities serviced, with rare exceptions, only Whites. According to Howard N. Rabinowitz, what emerged "was a shift from a policy of exclusion to one of segregation."[53] The Bureau even had to pay some local governments to accept freedmen in local facilities. This cajoling or forcing of local governments to provide health and other social services to freedmen became a common practice throughout the South.[54]

However, once the Freedmen's Bureau left an area, segregated health facilities became the rule. Todd L. Savitt noted "Once the Bureau was gone . . ., freedmen had no system of health care upon which to rely. Hospitals and dispensaries were left in the hands of White officials and White doctors."[55] Freedmen remained dependent on the largess of Whites then as they had been as slaves before. The Freedmen's Hospital in Washington, D.C.,was the only facility to remain open after the Bureau ceased its medical activities.[56] The South established and maintained for Blacks separate asylums, poorhouses, institutions for the deaf and dumb, homes for children, and adjuncts to city and county hospitals and infirmaries.

Thus, federal policy paved the way for the adoption of segregated hospital facilities by municipal governments, especially in the South. Private hospitals were strictly for Whites and in some cities, such as Atlanta, the municipality paid private hospitals to take care of indigent Blacks.[57] By the late 1800s only a very few city and private hospitals provided care to Blacks, such as the College of Infirmary of the Hampden-Sydney Medical Department in Richmond, Virginia (later named Medical College of Virginia), Bellevue Hospital (Richmond), and Montoeri Hospital (Petersburg).[58] In nearly all instances, the wards were segregated by race. In the early 1890s municipal hospitals in Atlanta and Nashville opened segregated wards with separate entrances for Blacks.[59] Rabinowitz observed that "by

1890 the announced goals of the Southern welfare policy was the acceptance of Blacks in institutions on the basis of separate but equal treatment."[60] It was not until 1891 that the first major hospital was established for Blacks that was owned and controlled by Blacks. In that year, Provident Hospital and Nurses Training School was founded in Chicago.

CONCLUSION

It is difficult to assess the overall effectiveness of the Freedmen's Bureau health program on the health status of former slaves. Accounts of Black health status show that during the early years of the Reconstruction era the Black mortality rate was about twice that of Whites. In 1868 the rate of deaths among Blacks was 32.42 deaths per 1,000 while among Whites it was 16.53 per 1,000.[61] Differentials in infant mortality between Blacks and Whites were even greater. By the 1870s numerous cities in the South--such as Charleston, New Orleans, Memphis, Savannah, Augusta, Atlanta, Mobile, and Richmond--reported the mortality rate of Blacks to be two to three times higher than that of Whites.[62] Donald Henderson wrote "It was not possible . . . for the efficient operation of the Freedmen's Bureau to reach the whole mass of the suffering freedmen" [and] "As the Negroes became more and more dependent upon themselves, the lack of medical facilities, their carelessness in administering remedies or in following the advice of physicians, the congestion in unsanitary quarters and the lack of wholesome food--all of these factors produced among the freedmen an appalling number of deaths."[63] Thus, while the Freedmen's Bureau did provide some health care and hospital services to former slaves, societal conditions in which the freedmen found themselves did not complement the Bureau's activities. In addition, freedmen as a whole, had little knowledge of proper health and medical care, sanitation, and dietary requirements.

NOTES

1. Mary Louise Marshall, "Plantation Medicine." *Bulletin of the Medical Library Association* 26 (3) (January 1938): 115-128.
2. Weymouth T. Jordan, "Plantation Medicine in the Old South." *The Alabama Review* 3 (April 1950): 83-107.

3. Richard H. Shryock, "Medical Practice in the Old South." *The South Atlantic Quarterly* 29 (April 1930): 160-178.

4. Cited in "Affect's Cotton Plantation Record and Account Book--Duties of an Overseer." *DeBow's Review* 18 (1855): 339-345.

5. See R. S. Weston, "Management of a Southern Plantation." *DeBow's Review* 22 (1857): 38-44; W. B. Blanton, *Medicine in Virginia in the Eighteenth Century* (1931); and Marshall, "Plantation Medicine," p. 121.

6. James Ewell, *Planter's and Mariner's Medical Companion* (Philadelphia: John Bioren, 1807). Cited in Marshall, "Plantation Medicine," p. 124.

7. Professional White physicians and non-professional medical practitioners were quite interested in slave health because of the view that slaves were physiologically and anatomically different from Whites and/or were susceptible or immune to certain ailments and diseases. Leading medical periodicals in the antebellum South published numerous articles on Black/slave differences in physiology/anatomy, disease susceptibility, or disease immunity. See, for example, *Southern Medical and Surgical Journal* (1836-1867), *Western Journal of Medicine and Surgery* (1840-1855), *New Orleans Medical News and Hospital Gazette* (1854-1861), and *Charleston Medical Journal and Review* (1846-1860). Some other medical journals during this time were *Southern Medical Reports*, *Southern Journal of Medicine and Pharmacy*, and *The American Journal of Medical Sciences*.

8. Marshall, "Plantation Medicine," p. 121.

9. See H. I. Catteral, *Judicial Cases Concerning American Negroes II.* (Washington, DC: 1929), pp. 43, 144, 520-521.

10. Ibid., pp. 520-521.

11. Martha Carolyn Mitchell, "Health and the Medical Profession in the Lower South, 1845-1860." *Journal of Southern History* 10 (1944): 424-446.

12. Todd L. Savitt, *Medicine and Slavery: The Diseases and Health Care of Blacks in Antebellum Virginia* (Urbana, IL: University of Illinois Press, 1978).

13. Shryock, "Medical Practice in the Old South," pp. 172-173.

14. V. A. Moody, *Slavery on Louisiana Sugar Plantations* (New York: AMS Press, 1976).

15. Ibid., p. 54.

16. See Moody, *Slavery on Louisiana Sugar Plantations*; and W. D. Postell, *The Health of Slaves on Southern Plantations* (Baton Rouge, LA: Louisiana State University Press, 1951).

17. C. S. Sydnor, "Life Span of Mississippi Slaves," *American Historical Review* 35 (1930): 566-576.

18. Postell, *The Health of Slaves on Southern Plantations*, pp. 134-136.

19. Ibid., pp. 136-138.

20. Ibid., pp. 135-136.

21. R. W. Fogel and S. E. Engerman, *Time on the Cross: The Economics of American Negro Slavery* (Boston: Little Brown, 1974): 120.

22. Ibid., p. 120.

23. Postell, *The Health of Slaves on Southern Plantations*, p. 139.

24. Ibid., p. 139.

25. Ibid., pp. 139-140.

26. M. A. Cooke, *The Health of Blacks During Reconstruction* (University of Maryland, Ph.D. Dissertation, 1983).

27. Shryock, "Medical Practice in the Old South," p. 173.

28. H. Belz, "The Freedmen's Bureau Act of 1865 and the Principle of No Discrimination According to Color." *Civil War History* 21 (September 1975): 197-217.

29. J. Thomas May, "A 19th Century Medical Care Program for Blacks: The Case of the Freedmen's Bureau." *Anthropological Quarterly* 46 (3) (July 1973): 160-171.

30. Cooke, *The Health of Blacks During Reconstruction*, p. 163.

31. Gaines M. Foster, "The Limitations of Federal Health Care for Freedmen, 1862-1868." *Journal of Southern History* 68 (August 1982): 349-372.

32. Ibid., p. 364.

33. For a general discussion on the history of the dispensary in the United States see Charles E. Rosenberg, "Social Class and Medical Care in 19th Century America: The Rise and Fall of the Dispensary." *Journal of the History of Medicine and Allied Sciences* 29 (1974): 32-54; and Michael M. Davis, Jr., and Andrew R. Warner, *Dispensaries: Their Management and Development* (New York: Macmillan, 1918).

34. Foster, "The Limitations of Federal Health Care for Freedmen," p. 364.

35. Ibid., p. 364.
36. Ibid., p. 364.
37. Ibid., p. 365.
38. Ibid., p. 365.
39. Ibid., pp. 364-365. For a general discussion of the Freedmen's Bureau activities in Texas see Claude Elliot, "The Freedmen's Bureau in Texas." *The Southwestern Historical Quarterly* 56 (July 1952): 1-2.
40. Todd L. Savitt, "Politics in Medicine: The Georgia Freedmen's Bureau and the Organization of Health Care, 1865-1866." *Civil War History* 28 (1) (1982): 45-64.
41. Ibid., pp. 48-49.
42. Ibid., pp. 48-62.
43. Foster, "The Limitations of Federal Health Care for Freedmen," pp. 364-365.
44. Abbot, *The Freedmen's Bureau in South Carolina*, pp. 36-43.
45. Marshall Scott Legan, "Disease and Freedmen in Mississippi During Reconstruction" *Journal of the History of Medicine*, (July 1973): 257-267.
46. Alan Raphael, "Health and Social Welfare of Kentucky Black People, 1865-1870." *Societas, A Review of Social History*.
47. M.A. Cooke, *The Health of Blacks During Reconstruction* (Ph.D. Dissertation, University of Maryland, 1983), pp. 122-164.
48. Ibid., pp. 124-143.
49. Foster, "The Limitations of Federal Health Care for Freedmen," pp. 365.
50. Legan, "Disease and Freedmen in Mississippi During Reconstruction," p. 259
51. Howard N. Rabinowitz, "From Exclusion to Segregation: Health and Welfare Services for Southern Blacks, 1865-1890." *Social Service Review* (September 1974): 328 and Howard N. Rabinowitz, *Race Relations in the Urban South, 1865-1890* (New York: Oxford Press, 1978): pp. 128-151.
52. Rabinowitz, *Race Relations in the South*, pp. 140-144.
53. Rabinowitz, "From Exclusion to Segregation," p. 330.
54. Ibid., p. 330.
55. Savitt, "Politics in Medicine," p. 64.
56. Rabinowitz, "From Exclusion to Segregation," pp. 330-331.

57. Rabinowitz, "From Exclusion to Segregation," pp. 332-336.

58. Savitt, *Medicine and Slavery*, see Chapters 2 and 3.

59. Rabinowitz, *Race Relations in the South*, p. 138.

60. Ibid., p. 128.

61. Donald H. Henderson, *The Negro Freedmen* (NY: Cooper Square Publishers, 1971), p. 156.

62. Ibid., p. 156.

63. Ibid., p. 158.

2

The Black Hospital Movement: The Need for Hospitals, Training Clinics, and Medical Schools

Near the end of the nineteenth century Black physicians and other civic-social minded Blacks became concerned about the lack of adequate hospital facilities and religious and philanthropic organizations, and concerned Whites began to contribute to the development of Black hospitals and medical schools. The impetus for this movement was threefold. First, Black medical professionals needed Black hospitals and training clinics as a place to treat patients and as a professional gathering place to improve their skills through workshops, lectures, and training sessions. Second, Black community activists, educators, and social scientists, as well as physicians and concerned Whites, stressed that the lack of Black hospitals contributed to the poor health status of the Black community. Third, Black physicians saw Black hospitals as a larger part of a general movement to improve the social standing of Black people.[1]

Provident Medical Center in Chicago (initially named Provident Hospital and Training School) was founded in 1891 through the community leadership of Dr. Daniel Hale Williams, a noted Black physician, who approached the Black community about the feasibility of a hospital "where Blacks could be treated with dignity and study the medical profession."[2] The hospital graduated its first class of three Black nurses in 1893.[3] By 1900 there were about forty Black hospitals around the country, located in virtually every Southern state as well as in several Northern cities.[4] In Philadelphia, Dr. Nathan Mossell, the first Black to graduate from the University of Pennsylvania Medical School and the first Black to be admitted to the Philadelphia Medical Society, founded the Frederick Douglas's Memorial Hospital and Training School in 1895. Twelve years later, in 1907, four young

Black physicians founded Mercy Hospital in Philadelphia.[5] By 1910 there were some one hundred Black hospitals nationwide.[6] In 1912 Monroe Work, editor of the *Negro Year Book and Annual Encyclopedia of the Negro*, listed 63 hospitals and nurse training schools operated for Blacks. Table 2.1 points out these hospitals and training schools by state.

Yet, in the early twentieth century, for Blacks, finding an institution to receive professional medical training was a major problem. Over the 32-year period between 1868 and 1900, eleven Black medical colleges had provided such training.[7] The earliest of these institutions was Howard University Medical School, which opened to a diverse student body of eight in Washington, D.C. on November 9, 1868. Meharry Medical College, which admitted Blacks only, opened in Nashville, Tennessee in 1876.[8] By 1895, these institutions, along with several others, produced most of the 385 Black physicians in existence at the time.[9] Upon graduation an even greater problem existed for Black physicians that of finding acceptable internships in hospitals. While about 70 internships were available at Black hospitals in the 1920s, about one-third short of what was needed, only a handful of internships were available in segregated sections of Northern White hospitals.[10]

Of the 119 Black physicians who graduated in 1927 (87 percent from Howard and Meharry) 71, or 60 percent served internships in fourteen hospitals. Of these intern-ships, 68 were in twelve Black hospitals, with Freedmen's Hospital in Washington, D.C. having 24. At a minimum, thirty Black physicians were unable to find intern-ships.[11] In the South, internships at White hospitals were non-existent, although a few Southern hospitals would later establish segregated wards in the 1930s.[12] Table 2.2 points out the number of internships available to Black physicians in 1931 and 1936. Intern-ships increased by 27 during the 5-year period. The 1936 total represented an increase of some 40 percent from the 1920s. In 1931, there were 114 Black medical students for only 93 internships. In 1936 the number of internships was greater than the number of Black medical graduates, 120 internships to 73 medical graduates. The Depression at this time contributed to the decline in the number of Black medical graduates.

Table 2.1
Black Hospitals and Nurse Training
Schools by State, 1912

STATE	NUMBER
Alabama	6
District of Columbia	1
Florida	2
Georgia	5
Illinois	2
Indiana	3
Kansas	2
Louisiana	2
Maryland	1
Massachusetts	1
Missouri	2
North Carolina	5
Oklahoma	1
Ohio	1
Pennsylvania	3
South Carolina	3
Tennessee	8
Texas	6
Virginia	4
West Virginia	3
TOTAL	63

Source: Compiled from Monroe Work (ed.), *Negro Year Book and Annual Encyclopedia of the Negro* (Tuskegee, AL: Tuskegee Institute, 1912).

Further, Black physicians were also excluded from courses and fellowships offered by various public health departments and from seminars and training provided by medical associations.[13] As a result, Black physicians (in some cases with interested White physicians) created their own postgraduate programs at their own hospitals and colleges and offered training activities at their own professional associations. More than a hundred such associations were organized, including the National Medical Association (NMA) in 1895 in Atlanta, Georgia with its *Journal* beginning in 1909, the Old North State Medical Society of North Carolina in 1888, and the Lone Star Medical Association of Texas in 1886.[14] The NMA will celebrate its 100th anniversary in 1995.[15]

Dr. Daniel Hale Williams started the earliest Black teaching clinic in the South at Meharry Medical College. Dr. John Kenney started the John A. Andrew Clinics in 1912 at the John A. Andrew Hospital in Tuskegee, Alabama.[16] Dr. Clyde Bonnell offered postgraduate clinics at a Black academy of medicine in Durham, North Carolina in 1916.[17] Dr. George C. Hall of Provident Hospital (Chicago) traveled to the South (Alabama and Tennessee) in the early 1900s and provided surgical training and assistance to Black physicians.[18] Dr. Matilda A. Evans established three Black hospitals in South Carolina in the early 1900s as well as the Negro Health Association of North Carolina around 1916, which published the *Negro Health Journal*.[19] By the early 1920s several members of the NMA became concerned about the lack of hospital care for Blacks and the lack of hospitals where Black physicians could intern, train, and grow professionally.

THE NATIONAL HOSPITAL ASSOCIATION

In 1923, a small group of delegates attending the NMA Annual Meeting in St. Louis, Missouri formed the National Hospital Association (NHA) as a constituent member of NMA. The purpose of the organization, according to Kenney was to "bring to bear all forces possible in combating the unfavorable conditions existing relating to our (black) hospitals, practicing physicians, interns, and nurses."[20] Dr. H. M. Green was elected as President, Dr. J. H. Ward as Vice President, Dr. John A. Kenney as Executive Secretary, and Miss Petra Pinn, R.N. as Treasurer.[21] The NHA became a constituent

Table 2.2
Internships for Black Physicians
in Approved Hospitals, 1931 and 1936*

HOSPITALS	Number of Interns 1931	1936
John A. Andrews	2	2
Woodmen of Union	2	–
Freedmen's	24	24
Provident, Chicago	6	6
Flint Goodridge	4	4
Provident, Baltimore	7	8
Kansas City #2	12	12
City Hospital #2 (Homer G. Phillips)	15	40
St. Mary's Infirmary	–	4
Lincoln, NC	3	4
L. Richardson Mem.	2	2
St. Agnes	3	2
Frederick Douglass	3	–
Mercy, Philadelphia	5	5
Hubbard	5	6
Brewster	–	1
TOTAL (16)	93	120

Source: Based on data compiled in Numa P. G. Adams, "Sources of Supply of Negro Health Personnel: Physicians." Journal of Negro Education, pp. 468-476.
*Excludes internship data from Harlem Hospital and City Hospital, Cleveland.

member (Associate member) of the American Hospital Association and made contacts with the American Medical Association and the American College of Surgeons.[22] Interestingly, there were a number of individuals, particularly Black physicians in the North, who saw no need for such an organization. However, the editor of the Journal of the National Medical Association, Dr. J. A. Kenney, writing in 1926, noted that black doctors had no place to work as interns or practitioners "except in our own institutions."[23] Further, only eight Black hospitals that at the time were accredited for interns,[24] an increase of four hospitals since the formation of the NMA in 1923.[25]

With the closure of all Black medical schools except Howard and Meharry and their affiliated hospitals, the "Negro Medical ghetto" had begun to evolve. These two institutions and their hospitals, along with a few others, were where Black physicians served internships and obtained advanced training in residencies and specialties. The lack of approved Black hospitals for intern training led the editor of the *Journal of the National Medical Association* in 1926 to observe, "We do not agree with those who hold that racial hospitals are no necessity in the North because our patients are cared for in the White institutions. This condition may have obtained satisfaction years ago when members of our race seeking admission to the hospitals were few, but conditions have changed radically in the past ten years; and with the coming of members of the race by the scores of thousand into the Northern section, new problems have developed. We say unqualifiedly that racial hospitals are a distinct need for our patients, both in the North and in the South."[26]

Dr. Green in his 1927 president's address to the NHA pointed out that the eight Black hospitals accredited for intern training by the American Medical Association (AMA) accommodated 65 Black interns. Eight other Blacks were holding internships at a few other hospitals, including four at the Harlem Hospital, which had previously been closed to Black physicians. Sixteen other Blacks were interns at hospitals not yet classified by the AMA. In all, 89 Blacks were interns.[27]

Dr. Green estimated that approximately 200 Black hospitals existed in 1926/27, and he attempted to verify their existence by mail survey.[28] However, only 57 hospitals responded. With funding assistance of $5,000 from the Council on Medication Education of

AMA, the NHA decided to visit personally every Black hospital and conduct an "instructive survey."[29] A follow-up meeting was held with the AMA, the American Hospital Association, and the American College of Surgeons on August 12, 1926.[30] The personal visit survey was to be administered in 1930 by Dr. Algeron B. Jackson, former superintendent at Mercy Hospital in Philadelphia and former professor of public health at Howard University.[31] Dr. Jackson visited 120 hospitals and awarded each a grade of A, B, C, or D. Those that received a grade of D were viewed as basically worthless. Twenty-seven hospitals were graded D, and only 16 were graded A hospitals.[32] By geographic region, two "grade A" hospitals were located in Missouri and Pennsylvania, three in North Carolina, one each in Illinois, the District of Columbia, Tennessee, Alabama, Louisiana, and Maryland.[33] Dr. Jackson estimated that Black hospitals in the country were valued at some $50 million.[34] Dr. Green saw the NHA as becoming "not only a clearinghouse for hospital information and activities, but through roundtable discussions of hospital problems, should become a sort of post graduate school in hospitals development."[35]

At the 1927 meeting President Green recommended that the NHA "confer with the National Baptist Convention in their effort to inaugurate a number of denominational hospitals" and send a resolution of appreciation to the Associated Negro Press for "its liberal releases concerning our activities."[36] The NHA was granted an affiliate status with the AHA. However, the AHA made only a feeble attempt to deal with the problems of Black hospitals. An ad hoc committee on Hospitalization of Colored People established by the AHA in 1929 recommended that the NHA create the position of executive secretary (with AHA assistance) and establish a permanent office. Two years later, in 1931, the AHA voted not to commit to the NHA either financially or programmatically.[37] The NHA was unable to implement the recommendations of the AHA, unable to obtain major support from well-known White professional health associations or philanthropic foundations, and unable to enforce standardization requirements on Black hospitals.[38] Despite these shortcomings, the NHA has received much credit for leading its era into the "Negro Hospital Renaissance" or "the hospital awakening."[39]

PHILANTHROPY AND BLACK MEDICAL FACILITIES

In the early part of the twentieth century, several philanthropic organizations expressed interest in problems faced by Blacks, particularly in the areas of education and health. The General Education Board (GEB), the Phelps-Stokes Fund, the Slater Fund, the Jeanes Fund, the Duke Endowment, and the Julius Rosenwald Fund made financial contributions directly or indirectly to the health, education, and/or overall social progress of Blacks. Much of this support supported the building and modernization of Black hospitals. The contributions of the Julius Rosenwald Fund, the Duke Endowment, and the General Education Board are discussed below.

The Julius Rosenwald Fund. The Julius Rosenwald Fund was a substantial contributor to Black hospitals in particular and to Black health in general in rural health programs. Between 1929 and 1942 the Fund contributed a total of $1,691,928 to Black health activities.[40] The Fund was organized by incorporation in the State of Illinois in 1917 (to 1936) and centered its attention on human relations. It primarily focused on "discrimination against all peoples, Jews, Negroes, Catholics, Mexicans...." Among its stated purposes was "promotion of Negro schools and Negro welfare generally."[41] The Fund was especially concerned about the state of affairs in medical education for Blacks. It recognized that while the two medical schools at the time--Meharry Medical School in Nashville and Howard Medical School in Washington--were sorely needed, their ability to offer training of the highest quality was hampered by the lack of adequate funding.[42] The general strategy of the Black health program of the Fund as it related to Black hospitals and clinics was to "aid in developing a limited number of hospitals for Negroes, conducted demonstration of high standards and as training centers for Negro physicians, nurses, and administrators."[43]

The Julius Rosenwald Fund contributed $562,000 to 16 Black hospitals and clinics and an additional $615,500 to three Black hospitals designated as centers for special development. These three latter hospitals were Flint-Goodridge Hospital in New Orleans ($42,500), John A. Andrews Hospital in Tuskegee ($64,500), and Provident Hospital in Chicago ($508,500). The Fund also spent $300,000 on the development of Black health professional personnel

Table 2.3
Julius Rosenwald Fund Contributions to Black Hospitals

HOSPITAL	LOCATION	AMOUNT
Provident Hospital	Chicago	$130,614
Flint-Goodrich Hospital	New Orleans	4,575
Provident Hospital	Baltimore	24,629*
Mercy Hospital	Philadelphia	31,076
Knoxville Hospital	Knoxville, TN	50,000
Charity Hospital	Savannah, GA	50,000
State Negro Sanitarium	Arkansas	8,000
Dixie Hospital	Hampton, VA	99,045
St. Phillips Hospital	Richmond, VA	40,000
Good Samaritan Hospital	Charlotte, NC	15,000
L. Richardson Memorial Hospital	Greensboro, NC	17,000
St. Agnes Hospital	Raleigh, NC	15,000
Spartanburg General Hospital	Spartanburg, NC	40,000
Toumey Hospital	Sumter, NC	25,000
Michael M. Shoemaker Center	Cincinnati	1,860
Harlem Birth Control Clinic	New York City	10,000
Red Cross Hospital**	Louisville, KY	16,000

Source: Compiled from Edwin R. Embre, *Julius Rosenwald Fund: Review of Two Decades 1917-1936* (Chicago: 1936) and "Red Cross Hospital, Louisville, KY," *National Negro Health News* (January/March 1950): 13.

*The Rosenwald Fund also provided $30,000 for maintenance, which was paid over a period of 5 years on a decreasing scale. See Michael David, "Three Negro Hospitals: Their Growth and Service." *The Modern Hospital* 39 (September 1932): 55.

with most of the funds going to further training and education of Black physicians.[44] Table 2.3 points out the financial assistance given by the Julius Rosenwald Fund to the maintenance and development of 16 Black hospitals between the years 1928 and 1936.

In 1919, the Fund made available to Black graduates in medicine six fellowships effective for the academic year 1920-21, "to pursue advanced studies in the fundamental medical sciences (pathology, bacteriology, physiology, pharmacology, physiological chemistry, etc.) under favorable conditions."[45] The fellowship award consisted of at least $1,200 for transportation, laboratory and tuition fees, books, and living expenses. The announcement of the fellowships was sent to 17 major schools of medicine that had Black medical students including Boston University Medical School, Yale University School of Medicine, Northwestern University Medical School, University of Illinois College of Medicine, Medical School of Harvard University, College of Physicians and Surgeons of Columbia University, and University of Michigan Medical School as well as Meharry and Howard University Medical Schools. At the time of the application period these 17 institutions had at least nine Black medical students in their fourth year of study.[46] For the 1920-21 academic year, four Black physicians were selected three of whom finished their medical studies at Howard or Meharry. The remaining awardees finished from Northwestern University Medical School.[47]

The Julius Rosenwald Fund created a Division of Negro Health in 1934. Midian O. Bousfield, a former president of the National Medical Association, who had received intern training at Freedmen's Hospital in 1914 and was vice president of a Chicago-based insurance company, was appointed director. The Fund's administration, including both its president and Bousfield, supported a segregated but equal hospital system, and financial support was provided for this purpose.[48] The Fund was also adamant that Blacks be placed on health department staffs and that the number of Black public health nurses be increased. By 1934 the Fund saw almost 175 Black nurses working in county health departments and private agencies.[49]

Julius Rosenwald, aware of the health conditions, sickness, and death rates of Blacks in Chicago suggested the creation of a great medical center and hospital to provide care to Blacks in Chicago. Mr. Rosenwald served as the honorary chairman of a campaign to provide a $3,000,000 medical center for blacks.[50] The contributions of the Fund, the Conrad Hubert Estate, the Public Utility Group of Chicago, and the General Education Board totaled over $2,000,000.[51] In addition, 3,236 Blacks of Chicago subscribed a total of $220,000 making this the largest subscription at the time for any purpose.[52] The proposed new medical center was expected to provide high quality medical care, instructions for medical students, an increase in the number of internships for Black doctors, advanced training for Black doctors, and research opportunities.[53] Subsequently, a new Provident Hospital was opened.

The General Education Board. The General Education Board (GEB) was formed by John D. Rockefeller, Jr., and others in 1902 and chartered in 1903 to assist and promote education in the South for Blacks and Whites. The GEB was very concerned about education for Southern Blacks.[54] It provided monetary support for both Black public education and college training. College training would be "provided for carefully selected Negroes who will lead the race in the efforts to educate and improve itself."[55] In the area of health, the GEB provided medical training fellowships to selected Blacks and provided funds to selected Black hospitals. Substantial contributions were made to Provident Hospital in Chicago and Flint-Goodridge Hospital in New Orleans.[56]

The GEB gave $130,000 of the $500,000 (the federal government gave $370,000) needed to build and equip a new medical school building at Howard University in the 1920s and $250,000 toward $500,000 for an endowment.[57] In 1912, the Dean of Howard University School of Medicine, Edward A. Balloch, M.D., requested financial support from the GEB.[58] Dr. Abraham Flexner of GEB visited the medical school and hospital to inspect the buildings and equipment and the overall financial situation on October 24, 1919. Dr. Flexner's report, along with an on site visitation on December 17, 1919, by the Council on Medical Education of the American Medical Association, recommended that the medical school be generously supported.[59] In 1927 the Howard University Medical School had 220 students enrolled in medicine, 60 in pharmacy and 82 in dentistry.[60] In November 1929, the Board approved $5,000 for the library at Howard Medical School for the purchase of books and periodicals.[61]

In 1929 the Board provided $42,000 to support the salary and expenses of the dean of Howard University Medical School (Dr. Numa P. G. Adams) for five years and in February 1936 the Board provided $100,000 over a five-year period to support clinical teaching in the Departments of Medicine and Surgery at the Medical School.[62] By 1942, the GEB had appropriated a total of $633,959.45 to the Howard Medical School, supporting endowment salaries, construction, equipment, and training.[63]   The GEB also supported clinical fellowships at Meharry and gave $1.5 million for construction of Meharry's new plant.[64]

The Duke Endowment. The Duke Endowment was created in 1926 by James Buchanan Duke of North Carolina tobacco fame to aid in the long term improvement of White and Black hospitals in North Carolina and South Carolina.   The Endowment also created orphanages for the poor and established a new university and medical school. For hospitals, the Endowment furnished capital and operating grants and assistance in administration and finance. About one-third of the Endowment's income went toward hospital maintenance and operations.[65]

The Endowment began awarding hospital grants in January 1926 and by 1930 had assisted Black hospitals in both the Carolinas. Blacks in segregated White hospitals also benefitted from the Endowment's contributions to these facilities. Additional beds were added in both Black and White wards at these institutions.[66] In fact, the Endowment favored the development of Black units and wards in mixed hospitals.[67] Nevertheless, the Endowment provided some $1.2 million to support the operating expenses of twenty-two Black general hospitals in the Carolinas and about $130,000 for capital expenses at seven of these facilities.[68] The Endowment and the Julius Rosenwald Fund jointly supported projects at five Black hospitals.[69]   The Endowment contributed toward the building support of the Hospital and Training School for Nurses in Charleston, Good Samaritan Hospital in Charlotte, L. Richardson Memorial Hospital in Greensboro, and St. Agnes Hospital in Raleigh.[70]

Private and Individual Philanthropy

Major philanthropic organizations were not the only supporters of the growth and development of Black hospitals. Support also came from various other organizations and individuals. In New Orleans, the quest for a new Flint-Goodridge Hospital saw Blacks subscribe to $117,000, more than twice the amount they expected to raise. Also, the Board of Education of the Methodist Episcopal Church and the American Missionary Society contributed $500,000 each.[71] In North Carolina, the Women's Auxiliary of the Protestant Episcopal Church contributed to a new nurse's home at St. Agnes Hospital.[72] L. Richardson Memorial Hospital in Greensboro, North Carolina began with a donation of land from Matheson-Wills-Benbow Real Estate Company and donations of $10,000 and $50,000 from Mrs. Emanuel Sternberger and Mrs. L. Richardson, respectively.[73] In Alabama, the John A. Andrew Memorial Hospital was originally established as a gift from Mrs. Elizabeth A. Mason of Boston, who gave the building as a memorial to her paternal grandfather, John A Andrew, War Governor of Massachusetts. The building was valued at over $100,000. In the late 1920s Mrs. Mason gave $25,000 for building and equipment for a new annex.[74] At Provident Hospital in Chicago a contribution by the Robert R. McCormick Fund led to the installation of diagnostic and therapeutic X-ray units in the early 1960s.[75]

WHITE HOSPITAL SEGREGATION AND THE CONTINUING NEED FOR BLACK HOSPITALS

By 1930 there were some 183 Black hospitals in the United States.[76] By the end of 1932 there was one Black hospital for every 107,127 Blacks or one hospital bed for every 999 Blacks. For Whites the ratio was one hospital for every 18,737 Whites or one bed for every 110 Whites. For each Black physician only 1.1 hospital beds were available, in contrast to 6.7 beds for every White physician.[77] Most Black hospitals were located in the South where the availability of hospital beds and services for Blacks was at a minimum.[78] Yet, in the state of Mississippi the lack of hospital beds for Blacks was most acute. In the early 1930s only 65 beds were available for a population of about 1,000,000 Blacks, and there were only 69 Black physicians.

In Texas the conditions were almost similar: There were 136 beds for some 850,000 Blacks.[79]

Survey findings from 711 hospital administrators in 18 Southern and border states and the District of Columbia administered by the Southern Conference Educational Fund in 1952 reflected widespread segregation and inequities in hospital care between Blacks and Whites.[80]   While 584 hospitals (82 percent) reportedly admitted Blacks, only 32.4 percent of the beds were available to Blacks. About 406 of the hospitals admitted Blacks on a segregated basis. Respondent administrators were also asked what racial policies they favored in their hospitals (without segregation, Plan A; with segregation, Plan B; separate hospitals, Plan C; or other). Table 2.4 shows these responses by state.   A large number of the respondent administrators favored Plan B (with segregation).   About 93 and 86 percent of the respondent administrators from Louisiana and Alabama, respectively, favored Plan B.   Between 70 to 76 percent of the respondents from Arkansas, Delaware, Georgia and Mississippi favored Plan B (with segregation).   Interestingly, a number of respondents indicated that they personally preferred that their hospital practice Plan A (without segregation). The following comments are illustrative of this point.

From a hospital administrator at a large religious institution in Missouri:

I am confident that the time will come when segregation in hospitals will be eliminated. Having separate hospitals for each makes this difficult at present. We shall strive to be Christian in our efforts to destroy discrimination. I do not believe a divided, segregated hospital is our immediate answer to the fact that Negroes are now not admitted except for emergencies.[81]

From a Tennessee hospital administrator:

Segregation should not be mandatory in case of need. The primary purpose of the hospital, to relieve pain and suffering due to illness or injury, should never be clouded nor forgotten.[82]

From an unidentified respondent:

As an individual I would prefer Plan A. However, as our
community is definitely segregated, Plan B is the only possible one
at this time.[83]

The survey findings also revealed that hospital care for Blacks in one
unnamed Texas city was hypothetical because it was nonexistent. This
community of 3,000 did not allow Blacks to participate in any activity
or function in the city, not even as laborers or servants.[84]

A few years later survey findings reported by Cornely from
hospitals in eight Southern cities in seven states indicated that only 6
percent (4 of 69 hospitals) of general hospitals admitted Blacks without
restrictions; about one-third did not admit any Blacks; and
approximately half had segregated wards.[85] In North Carolina, for
example, only about 20 percent of all hospital beds in the state were
available to Blacks, approximately one bed for every 840 Blacks.[86] By
1943, 5 Catholic hospitals existed exclusively for Black patients; three
were located in Alabama. The five hospitals were Holy Family
Hospital in Ensley, Alabama; Martins Porres Maternity Hospital in
Mobile, Alabama; Holy Ghost Home for Incurables in Marbury,
Alabama; St. Mary's Hospital in St. Louis, Missouri; Holy Cross
Hospital, Austin, Texas. A sixth Catholic hospital, St. Jude's Catholic
Hospital for Negroes, was to be established in Montgomery,
Alabama.[87]

The Southern Conference Education Fund compiled a twenty year
account of incidents from testimony and media reports in which
segregated White hospitals refused to provide adequate emergency care
or provided no care at all to Blacks.[88] Below are a few summarized
incidents.

In the fall of 1930, a Black man was injured in an automobile
accident near Huntsville, Alabama. After being taken to Huntsville,
he was advised that no hospital facilities were available for Blacks and
the closest available care was ten miles away in Athens, Alabama.
The victim died en route. On November 6, 1931, a dean at Fisk
University and a female student were critically injured in an
automobile accident near Dalton, Georgia. Three White physicians
administered first aid treatment in their homes and then took them to

Table 2.4

Number and Percentage of Southern Hospital Administrators
Favoring Each of Three Alternatives Relative to Racial
Policies in Hospitals in the South by State

STATE	PLAN A Without Segregation		PLAN B With Segregation		PLAN C Separate Hospitals		OTHER AND BLANK		TOTAL
Alabama	3	8	30	86	2	6	..	..	36
Arkansas	3	15	13	70	2	10	1	5	19
Delaware	1	13	6	74	1	13	..	..	8
D. C.	3	75	1	25	0	..	..	..	4
Florida	6	11	34	64	9	17	4	8	53
Georgia	0	..	27	75	6	17	3	8	36
Kentucky	12	26	23	51	4	10	6	13	45
Louisiana	0	..	26	93	2	7	..	..	28
Maryland	8	33	13	55	2	8	1	4	24
Mississippi	0	..	19	76	2	8	4	16	25
Missouri	14	37	14	37	2	5	8	21	38
New Mexico	16	59	5	19	..	..	6	22	27
North Carolina	4	10	24	58	12	30	1	2	41
Oklahoma	9	21	26	62	2	5	5	12	42
South Carolina	1	5	13	62	4	19	3	14	21
Tennessee	6	15	25	61	5	12	5	12	41
Texas	23	15	98	67	13	9	13	9	147
Virginia	5	12	26	63	4	10	6	15	41
West Virginia	11	32	16	46	4	11	4	11	35

Source: James A. Dombrowski, "Practices and Attitudes in Southern Hospitals." *The Modern Hospital* 79 (2) (August 1952): 79. Reprinted with permission from MODERN HEALTHCARE. Copyright Crain Communications, Inc., 740 N. Rush Street, Chicago, IL.

"a house where Negroes are sent in emergencies." The doctors did not consider taking the two to the nearby White hospital, Hamilton Memorial Hospital at Dalton. An ambulance had to be summoned from Chattanooga, Tennessee, 66 miles away, to take them to Chattanooga hospital. Both died within 24 hours.

In March 1932 a Black girl suffering from a serious bullet wound was denied admission to two Washington, D.C., hospitals-Sibley Hospital and Homeopathic Hospital. She was dead on arrival at Freedmen's Hospital. In March 1937 a Black female was taken to Knickerbocker Hospital in New York City suffering from a cerebral hemorrhage. The attending physician had phoned the hospital in advance providing symptoms and diagnosis. The patient's admission was delayed once it was discovered she was Black. She was admitted more than a hour later, then died.

On April 25, 1947, two students of Clark College (a Black college) were seriously injured in an automobile accident near Pelhma, Tennessee. An ambulance took the two 14 miles to a hospital in Manchester, Tennessee, where they were denied admission on the grounds that the hospital was full. They were then carried 30 miles to the hospital at the University of the South, where they received only first aid because the hospital indicated it was full. Finally, they were able to receive treatment at a hospital 50 miles from the scene of the accident in Fayetteville, Tennessee.

In February 1951 a high school basketball player suffering from sugar diabetes was refused admission to Akron, Ohio, City Hospital because the hospital while not segregated did not "mix" its semiprivate rooms. The patient died in the emergency room five hours later. In October 1951 a woman in labor was sent home from John Gaston Hospital in Memphis, Tennessee, after a doctor informed her she was "in the early stages of labor." Upon arriving home, she gave birth to twins on the front porch, unable to reach her bed. One baby died of strangulation by umbilical cord. The city-owned institution had a policy of treating Black maternity cases as outpatients.[89]

THE GROWTH OF BLACK HOSPITALS

Although Black hospitals in the segregated South were founded with the finest and highest intentions to render a most needed and helpful service, survey findings of 125 Black hospitals led Jackson to remark, "they miss[ed] the mark because of untrained and ignorant management, lack of professional cooperation, petty jealousies . . ., poor equipment, lack of wholesome atmosphere within and without, and . . . inadequate skill to do the job."[90] The findings also revealed the need for Black hospitals to have outpatient departments, a mostly neglected service for Blacks, especially in the South, and better selection and training of Black nurses by having Black nurse-training schools. According to Jackson, "there is nothing quite so important as the creation and preservation of efficient out-patient clinics."[91] In the area of Black hospital nurse training schools, Jackson was critical of the inadequate education of "many little country and small town girls" who were sought after and selected for training by these institutions. Jackson noted that the "'diploma' issued them by these 'training schools' [did] not permit them to enter upon the examination of their state to try for the coveted degree 'Registered Nurse'".[92]

In 1942 there were some 110 Black hospitals representing an increase of about 5,838 new beds since the late 1930s. The largest increase in the new beds (60 percent) were for the insane. The remaining new beds were in general hospitals, tuberculosis sanitaria and other specialized hospitals.[93] By 1944 only 124 hospitals in the country exclusively served Black patients.[94] An increase of 14 from 1942.[95] These hospitals had about 20,800 beds, including 800 bassinets, and were located in 23 states and Washington, D.C.[96] Table 2.5 provides a listing of the number of Black hospitals by state. Interestingly, the non-Southern states of Michigan and Missouri were identified as having ten and seven Black hospitals, respectively. North Carolina, Virginia, and Florida were identified as the Southern states with the largest number of Black hospitals: 13, 10, and 11, respectively. A large number of the hospitals (112) were operated by nongovernmental groups (church, fraternal, community, proprietary); the remainder (12) were operated by federal, state, or municipal governments. The *National Negro Health News*, published by the U.S. Public Health Service in 1946, indicated that the Southern states of North Carolina and Georgia had the largest number of beds for Black patients, 2,519 and 1,659 respectively.[97] However, in a finding similar to those of Jackson years earlier, the Commission on Hospital Care in 1947 noted that only about one-third of the Black hospitals identified had received recognition of some kind by some professional specialty organization, such as the American College of Surgeons or the Council on Medical Education and Hospitals of the American Medical Association.[98]

Further, by 1947 only 18 hospitals offered approved internships for Black physicians: 10 Black hospitals and Harlem and Sydenham Hospitals (New York City), City Hospital (Cleveland, Ohio), Cook County Hospital (Chicago), U.S. Marine Hospital (Boston), Receiving Hospital (Detroit), Los Angeles County Hospital, and Jersey City Hospital (New Jersey). Also, only 116 residences and assistant residences were available to Black physicians at 17 hospitals. Seventy-four of them were at four of the leading Black hospitals at the time Freedmen's, Homer G. Phillips, Provident (Chicago) and Hubbard.[99]

The Commission on Hospital Care, established in 1944 by the American Hospital Association, sought to assess the number of hospitals and public health facilities, to identify problems of hospital care in the United States, to determine the overall need for additional facilities, and service and to formulate a coordinated national plan for hospital service.[100] Because of the peculiarity of the Black hospital problem, the Commission devoted a separate chapter. Among its recommendations were the following:

1. That adequate and competent hospital care should be available without restriction to all people regardless of race, creed, color or economic status.

Table 2.5
Geographic Distribution of Black Hospitals by State, 1945

STATE	NUMBER
Alabama	9
Arkansas	5
Washington, D.C.	3
Florida	11
Georgia	8
Illinois	2
Indiana	2
Kansas	3
Louisiana	1
Michigan	10
Maryland	4
Delaware	1
Mississippi	4
Missouri	7
New Jersey	1
North Carolina	13
New York	1
Oklahoma	4
Pennsylvania	3
South Carolina	7
Tennessee	4
Texas	7
Virginia	10
West Virginia	4

Source: Eugene H. Bradley, "Health, Hospitals and the Negro,"
Modern Hospital 65 (August 1945): 43-44.

2. That facilities for the care of Negro patients should be provided in hospitals that serve White patients rather than in separate hospitals. In these communities in which segregation is required by law, as good hospital service should be maintained for Negro patients as is provided for White patients.[101]

At the time of the Commission's findings, Black hospitals numbered 20,800 beds out of a national total of 1,700,000.[102]

The Southern Conference Educational Fund in 1952 reported survey findings from a poll conducted of 2414 medical institutions in 18 Southern and border states and the District of Columbia regarding hospital patient segregation and hospital administrators' racial policy preferences best suited for the health needs of their communities.[103] From 711 responses (29 percent), it was revealed that 584 (82 percent) representing 33,451 beds (32 percent) admitted Blacks as patients. However, more than two-thirds of the beds available to Blacks were fixed by quota. Not surprisingly, about 62 percent of the respondent hospital administrators favored the admission of Blacks on a segregated basis, while 10 percent favored separate hospitals for Whites and Blacks.[104]   Because the complete findings of the survey were not reported, it is not known which hospitals responded.

NOTES

1. Vanessa Northington Gamble, *The Black Community Hospital* (New York: Garland Publishing, Inc., 1989), pp. 24-27.

2. "Provident-Chicago Celebrates 95th Anniversary." *The NRW Report* (June 1986): 3-5.

3. Daniel H. Williams, "The Need of Hospitals and Training Schools for the Colored People of the South." *Church Review* 17 (1) (July 1900): 9-19.

4. David McBride, *Integrating the City of Medicine: Blacks in Philadelphia Health Care*, 1910-1965 (Philadelphia: Temple University Press, 1989), pp. 8-9.

5. Ibid., p. 9.

6. Ibid., p. 9 and M.O. Bousfield, "An Account of Physicians of Color in the United States." *Bulletin of the History of Medicine* 17 (1) (January 1945): 61-84.

7. Herbert M. Morais, *The History of the Negro in Medicine* (New York: Publishers Co., Inc., 1967), p. 60. Interestingly, at least four other medical schools were opened for Blacks in Tennessee. Perhaps this may be explained by the widespread interest of Black and White philanthropic organizations in Tennessee.

8. Some other Black medical schools were, Flint Medical College (New Orleans), Leonard Medical College (Raleigh), Knoxville Medical College (Knoxville), Medical Department of the University of West Tennessee (Memphis), Louisville National Medical College (Louisville), Lincoln University Medical College (Oxford, Pennsylvania), Hannibal Medical College (Memphis), and Chattanooga National Medical College (Chattanooga). Several of these hospitals did not graduate any Black physicians because of their brief period of operation. See Leonard W. Johnson, "History of the Education of Negro Physicians," *Journal of the National Medical Association* 42 (1967): 439-446; and Morais, *The History of the Negro in Medicine*, pp. 30-42.

9. Morais, *The History of the Negro in Medicine*, pp. 40-44.

10. "Negro Doctors and Hospitals." *Opportunity* 3 (1925): 227-228.

11. Bousfield, "An Account of Physicians of Color in the United States," p. 78.

12. Paul B. Cornely, "Race Relations in Community Health Organizations." *American Journal of Public Health* 36 (September 1946): 984-992.

13. Paul B. Cornely, "Trends in Public Health Activities Among Negroes in 96 Southern Counties." *American Journal of Public Health* 32 (October 1942): 117-1124; and Paul B. Cornely, "Trends in Public Health Activities Among Negroes in 96 Southern Counties

During the Period 1930-1939: The Employment of Negro Professional Personnel." *Journal of the National Medical Association* 34 (January 1942): 3-11.

14. Morais, *The History of the Negro in Medicine*, pp. 57-58.

15. Although the *Journal of the National Medical Association* is nearly 100 years old, *The Medical and Surgical Observer*, first published in December 1892, was the first Black medical journal. The journal was founded by Black physician Dr. M. V. Lynk of Jackson, Tennessee, and lasted eighteen months. See Bousfield, "An Account of Physicians of Color in the United States," p. 70.

16. William Montague Cobb, "John A. Kenney, M.D." *Journal of the National Medical Association* 42 (1950): 175 and "Editorials-- Supplementary Medical Education: The John A. Andrew Clinical Society." *Journal of the National Medical Association* 33 (1) (January 1941): 32-33. See also Edward H. Beardsley, "Making Separate, Equal: Black Physicians and the Problems of Medical Segregation in the Pre-World War II South." *Bulletin of the History of Medicine* 57 (Fall 1983): 382-396.

17. Edward H. Beardsley, *A History of Neglect: Health Care for Blacks and Mill Workers in the Twentieth Century South* (Knoxville, TN: University of Tennessee Press, 1987).

18. "A Prominent Colored Physician." *Colored American Magazine* 14 (1908): 481.

19. Beardsley, *A History of Neglect*, pp. 53-62.

20. John A. Kenney, "The Negro Hospital Renaissance." *Journal of the National Medical Association* 22 (3) (July/September 1930): p. 109-112.

21. Ibid., pp.109-111.

22. Ibid., pp. 110-112; and Editorial, "An Important Conference," *Journal of the National Medical Association* (July/September 1926): 139.

23. Editorial, "An Important Conference," p. 139.

24. H. M. Green, "President's Address: The National Hospital Association." *Journal of the National Medical Association* 19(1) (January/March 1927): 16-21.

25. H. M. Green, "Annual Address of the President of the National Hospital Association," *Journal of the National Medical Association* (April/June 1928): 90-93. For a view of a National Hospital Association Business Meeting see "Minutes of the National Hospital Association," *Journal of the National Medical Association* 22 (4) (1930): 227-230. In 1923 there were approximately 202 Black hospitals in operation, with an average size of less than 50 beds. See "National Hospital Association." *Journal of the National Medical Association* 15 (1923): 286.

26. Editorial, "Why a National Hospital Association?" *Journal of the National Medical Association* (July/September 1926): 138-139.

27. Ibid., pp. 17-18.

28. Ibid., p. 17.

29. Ibid., p. 18.

30. The American Medical Association was viewed as being very fair and cooperative in assisting Black hospitals in qualifying for its approval. The American College of Surgeons was seen as conducting fair surveys but practiced exclusion of Black physicians. See Bousfield, "An Account of Physicians of Color in the United States," p. 73.

31. Green, "President's Address," pp. 14-15.

32. Ibid., pp. 16-19; and A. B. Jackson, "Hospitals and Health." *Journal of the National Medical Association* 22 (3) (1930): 115-119. Dr. Green defined Grades A, B, C in the following way. "'A' grade-hospitals properly accredited for training interns; 'A minus'--those not so accredited, but deficient only in minor respects; 'B'--hospitals properly accredited for training nurses but not interns; 'B minus'--hospitals deficient in minor points for operating standard training schools . . .; 'C' would include the nondescript hospital attempting educational work but without proper facilities. 'C minus' would

include the purely mercenary and generally unworthy." See Green, "President's Address," p. 18.

33. H. M. Green, "A Brief Study of the Hospital Situation among Negroes." *Journal of the National Medical Association* 22 (3) (1930): 112-114. At its Third Annual meeting in 1925, the NHA issued some minimum standards for its member hospitals, which focused primarily on supervision, record keeping, and nurse training. Although these standards were not equal to those set forth by the American College of Surgeons, they were an attempt to provide guidance to small Black hospitals that, for the most part, averaged less than 50 beds. See "National Hospital Association's Minutes of Third Annual Session," *Journal of the National Medical Association* 17 (1925): 231; and Gamble, *The Black Community Hospital*, p. 29.

34. Jackson, "Hospitals and Health," p. 118.

35. Green, "President's Address," p. 21.

36. Green, "Annual Address," p. 93.

37. For a discussion on these points see William H. Walsh, "Report of the Committee on Hospitalization of Colored People." *Transactions of the American Hospital Association* 32 (1930): 53-61; and American Hospital Association, "Report of the Board of Trustees, September 28, 1931." *Transactions of the American Hospital Association* 32 (1930): 53-61.

38. Gamble, *The Black Community Hospital*, p. 33.

39. Kenney, "The Negro Hospital Renaissance," p. 109.

40. Julius Rosenwald Fund Archives, 1943-1949, Conference of Foundation officers with the Trustees of the Julius Rosenwald Fund, p. 18, Nov. 8, 1947, Box 212, Folder 2045, Rockefeller Archives Center.

41. Notes from JHP to KED in 1952, Box 212, Folder 2045, Rockefeller Archives Center.

42. Julius Rosenwald Fund, p. 19, Box 212, Folder 2045, Rockefeller Archives Center.

43. E. R. Embree, *Julius Rosenwald Fund: Review of Two Decades* (Chicago: Julius Rosenwald Fund, 1936); and E. R. Embree, *Investment in People: The Story of the Julius Rosenwald Fund* (New York: Harper, 1949).

44. Julius Rosenwald Fund, p. 18, Box 212, Folder 2045, Rockefeller Archives Center.

45. Letter from Abraham Flexer to Dr. John P. Sutherland, Boston University Medical School, September 11, 1919, Rosenwald Fellow Negro Medical Fellowships, 1919-1922, Box 702, Folder 7221, Rockefeller Archives Center.

46. "Negro Medical Students, 1919-1920," Julius Rosenwald Fund, Box 702, Folder 7221.

47. Letter from Abraham Flexner to Dr. R. R. Moton, Tuskeegee Institute, May 28, 1990, Julius Rosenwald Fund, Box 702, Folder 7221.

48. Embree, *Investment in People*, pp. 72-86.

49. M. O. Bousfield, "Reaching the Negro Community." *American Journal of Public Health* 24 (1934): 209-215. In 1930 the seven states of Arkansas, Delaware, Kentucky, Mississippi, North Carolina, West Virginia, and Alabama employed only one part-time Black physician, three employed 29 Black nurses, and one employed Black dentists or dental hygienists. See Paul B. Cornely, "Segregation and Discrimination in Medical Care." *American Journal of Public Health*, pp. 1074-1075.

50. "Items of Interest." *Journal of the National Medical Association* (January/March 1930): 61.

51. The Julius Rosenwald Fund solicited support from the General Education Board for Provident Hospital. See letter dated July 5, 1929, from Edwin R. Embree, President, to Dr. Richard M. Pierce, Rockefeller Foundation, General Education Board files, Box 699, Folder 7200, Rockefeller Archive Center. See also Box 700, File 7205 for communications between the GEB and the University of Chicago and GEB inter-office correspondence regarding assistance to

Provident Hospital.

52. J. Thomas Helsom, "The New Provident Hospital and Training School." *Journal of the National Medical Association* 22 (3) (1930): 128-130. See also "A New Chicago Hospital." *Crisis* (February 1930): 47-58.

53. "Items of Interest," p. 61. Of related interest is that the land and construction were donated by philanthropic individuals. See G. F. Richings, *Evidences of Progress among Colored People*, 12th ed. (Philadelphia: George S. Ferguson Co., 1905).

54. E.R. Brown, *Rockefeller Medicine Men* (Berkeley: University of California Press, 1979).

55. Ibid., p. 47.

56. R. B. Fosdick, *Adventure in Giving: The Story of the General Education Board* (New York: Harper and Row, 1962); and M. H. Goldstein and B. C. MacLean, "A Hospital That Serves as a Center of Negro Medical Education." *The Modern Hospital* 39 (November 1932): 65-70. For a discussion of the GEB Provident Hospital (Chicago) see General Education Board, Provident Hospital Reports and Pamphlets, Box 700, Folder 7205, Rockefeller Archive Center.

57. Memorandum from H. J. Thorkelson regarding Howard University, Washington, DC, February 6, 1928, General Education Board, Howard University School of Medicine, 1926-1929, Box 28, Folder 259, Rockefeller Archives Center.

58. See correspondence from Edward A. Balloch, Dean of the Harvard University School of Medicine to the GEB dated April 19, 1912 and September 25, 1912, Box 28, Folder 256, General Education Board Archives, Howard University School of Medicine, 1912-1914. See also, Memorandum from H. J. Thorkelson regarding Howard University, Washington, DC, February 6, 1928, General Education Board, Howard University School of Medicine, 1926-1929, Box 28, Folder 259, Rockefeller Archives Center.

59. Howard University School of Medicine site inspection, October 24, 1919; Notes on a Visit to the Medical Department of Howard

University, December 17, 1919; Memorandum Regarding the Medical Department, Howard University; Letter to Abraham Flexner from Dr. William Pepper, University of Pennsylvania Medical School, January 12, 1920. General Education Board, Howard University School of Medicine, 1915-1290, Box 28, Folder 257, Rockefeller Archives Center.

60. Memorandum from H. J. Thorkelson regarding Howard University, Washington, DC, February 6, 1928, General Education Board, Box 28, Folder 259.

61. General Education Board Inter-office Correspondence, April 17, 1930, Howard University School of Medicine, 1930-33, Box 28, Folder 260, Rockefeller Archives Center.

62. Letter from Dr. Warren Weaver of the Rockefeller Foundation to Dr. Elmer L. Sevringhaus of the State of Wisconsin General Hospital, October 16, 1936, General Education Board, Howard University School of Medicine, 1934-1939, Box 28, Folder 261.

63. See Grant In Aid to Howard University, Washington, D.C., Box 29, Folder 270, General Education Board, Howard University School of Medicine Research Fund, 1942-1947.

64. William Montague Cobb, "Progress and Portents for the Negro in Medicine." *The Crisis* (April 1948): 107-126.

65. E. H. Beardsley, *A History of Neglect: Health Care for Blacks and Mill Workers in the Twentieth Century South* (Knoxville, TN: University of Tennessee Press, 1987).

66. Ibid., pp. 33-45.

67. The Duke Endowment, *Annual Report of the Hospital Section, 1937* (Charlotte: The Endowment, 1938), p. 24.

68. Gamble, *The Black Community Hospital* (New York: Garland Publishing, Inc., 1989), p. 35.

69. Ibid., p. 37.

70. L. C. Downing, "Early Negro Hospitals." *Journal of the National Medical Association* 33 (January 1941): 13-18; and M. Ross, "Improved Negro Hospital Facilities Is Hopeful Sign for the South."

Modern Hospital (October 1932): 53-60.

71. "The History of Flint-Goodridge Hospital of Dillard University." *Journal of the National Medical Association* 61 (6) (November 1969): 533-536; and H. W. Knight, "Flint-Goodridge Hospital." *Journal of the National Medical Association* 22 (3) (1930): 130-131.

72. Lemuel T. Delany, "St. Agnes Hospital, Raleigh, North Carolina." *Journal of the National Medical Association* 22 (3) (1930): 135-136.

73. H. Sebastian, "L. Richardson Memorial Hospital." *Journal of the National Medical Association* 22 (3) (1930): 140-144; and W. Elkins, "The History of L. Richardson Memorial Hospital." *Journal of the National Medical Association* 61 (3) (May 1969): 205-212.

74. Eugene H. Dibble, Jr., and Ruth A. Ballard, "John A. Andrew Memorial Hospital." *Journal of the National Medical Association* 53 (2) (March 19691): 103-118; and Eugene H. Dibble, "The John A. Andrew Memorial Hospital, Tuskegee Institute, Alabama." *Journal of the National Medical Association* 22 (3) (1930): 137-138.

75. H. B. Matthews, "Provident Hospital: Then and Now." *Journal of the National Medical Association* 53 (3) (May 1961): 209-224.

76. Council on Medical Education and Hospitals, "Hospitals and Medical Care in Mississippi," *Journal of the American Medical Association*, 112 (June 3, 1939): 1317-1332.

77. N. P. G. Adams, "An Interpretation of the Significance of the Homer G. Phillips Hospitals." *Journal of the National Medical Association* 26 (1) (February 1934): 13-17.

78. Council on Medical Education and Hospitals, "Hospitals and Medical Care in Mississippi," pp. 2318-2320.

79. Adams, "An Interpretation of the Significance of Homer G. Phillips Hospitals," p. 15.

80. J. A. Dombrowski, "Practices and Attitudes in Southern Hospitals." *Modern Hospital* 79 (August, 1952): 78-79, 140 and

"Southern Hospital Facilities for Negroes." *The Survey* (April 1952): 178-179.

81. Ibid., p. 78.

82. Ibid., p. 79.

83. Ibid., p. 79.

84. Ibid., p. 79.

85. Paul B. Cornely, "Segregation and Discrimination in Medical Care in the United States." *American Journal of Public Health* 46 (September 1956): 1074-1081.

86. M. Ross, "Improved Negro Hospital Facilities Is Hopeful Sign for the South," pp. 54-58.

87. "Colored Hospitals." *The Commonwealth* 38 (1943): 593.

88. A. Mound, *The Untouchables: The Meaning of Segregation in Hospitals* (New Orleans: Southern Conference Education Fund, 1952).

89. On the above discussion see Mound, *The Untouchables*, pp. 15-36.

90. A. B. Jackson, "Hospitals and Health." *Journal of the National Medical Association* 22 (1930): 115-119.

91. Ibid., p. 117.

92. Ibid., p. 118.

93. E. H. Bradley, "Health, Hospitals, and the Negro." *Modern Hospital* 65 (August 1945): 43-44.

94. Ibid.

95. Ibid., pp. 43-44.

96. "Hospital Beds for Patients in Negro Hospitals by States." *National Negro Health News* (April/June 1946): 15.

97. *National Negro Health News* was a bulletin "for release of announcements and data pertaining to the National Negro Health Week and its year round sponsor, the National Negro Health Movement." The bulletin was published from 1933-1950. See "Memorandum of Transmittal," *National Negro Health News* (January/March 1933). For a history of the National Negro Health Week Movement see

Roscoe C. Brown, "The National Negro Health Week Movement."
Journal of Negro Education 6 (3) (1937): 553-564.

98. Commission on Hospital Care, "Provision of Hospital Service
and Quality Care for Negroes." In *Hospital Care in the United States*
(New York: The Commonwealth Fund), pp. 163-167.

99. William Montague Cobb, *Medical Care and the Plight of the
Negro* (New York: NAACP, 1947).

100. Commission on Hospital Care, "Provision of Hospital Service
and Quality Care for Negroes," p. 163.

101. Ibid., pp. 166-167.

102. "A Generation Behind." *Time* (April 7, 1947): 58.

103. Mound, *The Untouchables*, pp. 12-25.

104. Ibid., pp. 14-17.

3

Descriptions of
Selected Black Hospitals

The listing of black hospitals is arranged alphabetically by state and city.

THE COTTAGE HOME INFIRMARY

Decatur, Alabama

Opened in 1900 in a cottage of three rooms. Expanded to a two-story building of 18 rooms. In 1910, the first nurses in the nurses' training program. Both medical and surgical cases were treated in the institution.[1]

HOLY FAMILY HOSPITAL

Ensley, Alabama

Evolved from a little hut and a duplex to a 12-bed ward, chapel, and clinic to a 50-bed institution of three one-story framehouses founded by the Sisters of Charity in 1943. Provided care to about 200 outpatients per month. In 1946 handled maternity cases only. In July 1950 the citizens of Birmingham, Alabama, contributed $250,000 for a new facility which was dedicated in January 1954. By the early 1960s, 19 Black doctors comprised the active and associate staff.[2]

SAINT MARTIN DE PORRES HOSPITAL

Mobile, Alabama

The Martin de Porres Hospital can be traced to a small five bed maternity ward opened for Blacks in 1941. The hospital was named after Brother Martin de Porres, a saintly Black known as the "Wonder Worker of Peru." In 1942 the hospital was delegated to two Sisters of Mercy.   Shortly thereafter, an additional ward was added, increasing the bed capacity to nine. In 1949 the hospital received a Hill-Burton grant, expanding the facility to 100 beds. The total cost of the facility was $616,000.[3]

TUSKEGEE INSTITUTE HOSPITAL AND NURSE TRAINING SCHOOL

(Renamed John A. Andrew Memorial Hospital in 1912)
Tuskegee, Alabama
Founded in 1892 as a medical facility for students and faculty at Tuskegee Institute. By 1900 hospital facilities were extended to the community. Composed of two stories with an annex, which allowed space for 45 patients. Moved to a new building in 1913 and name changed to the John A. Andrew Memorial Hospital with male and female wards, surgical and isolation wards, convalescing rooms, obstetrical wards, diet kitchen on each floor, operating rooms, anesthetizing, sterilizing, and recovery rooms, a children's ward, five private rooms, emergency room, classrooms, and dining room. The hospital received a "Grade A" rating from the American College of Surgeons and was approved by the Council on Medical Education and Hospitals of the American Medical Association. A member of the American Hospital Association. By 1961 bed capacity had increased to 175.[4]

U. S. VETERANS' HOSPITAL #91 TUSKEGEE VETERANS ADMINISTRATION HOSPITAL

Tuskegee, Alabama
Formally dedicated during President Harding's Administration on February 12, 1923 and opened June 15, 1923 for the care of Black veterans. Vice President Calvin Coolidge represented the federal government at the dedication. The hospital consisted of 600 beds and was built and equipped at a cost of $2.5 million on 464 acres of land. Colonel Robert H. Stanley, a White, was made Superintendent. Plans were made to appoint a full White staff of both doctors and nurses. Each White nurse would be assigned a Black nurse-maid to prevent the White nurses from having contact with Black patients. By July 7, 1924, the hospital was operated by entirely Black personnel. Colonel Joseph Henry Ward was the first Black commanding officer.

The hospital itself occupied 320 acres and consisted of an administration building, a main infirmary building, six wards, a tuberculosis infirmary, two buildings for ambulant tuberculosis patients, an infirmary for ambulant neuro-psychiatric patients, a recreation building, a library, a nurses home, an attendant's building, a dietary building, an apartment building, and other buildings housing maintenance and support systems. The physical equipment was valued at nearly $3.4 million. The hospital had a capacity for nearly 750 patients and was rated "Class A" without reservation by the American College of Surgeons and the American Hospital Association.

During fiscal year 1929, the federal government spent $788,719 at the hospital including about $454,000 for salaries. By the late 1920s the number of patients treated annually was about 1,000. The professional staff (all Black) consisted of 23 physicians, 2 dentists, 1 pharmacist, 3 laboratory technicians, 3 physiotherapy aides, 7 occupational therapy aides, 2 librarians, 4 dieticians, and 52 nurses. By the early 1940s the bed capacity had increased to 1,558 and the number of employees was 621 including 25 physicians, 2 dentists, 67 nurses, 257 hospital attendants, 93 dietetic employees, and others.[5]

THOMAS C. McRAE MEMORIAL SANATORIUM

Alexander, Arkansas

McRae Sanitarium was established in 1931 by the Arkansas State legislature as an institution for Blacks suffering from tuberculosis. The institution grew from 26 beds to the largest, most complete institution of its kind in the United States. The hospital had 411 beds, a modern surgical unit, a nurses' home, male dormitory, quarters for married staff members, a fire station, and a rehabilitation center. A children's building and an auxiliary nurses' home building were added in 1960. In 1938 in-training courses for staff were inaugurated. A course in nurse training was started in 1940.[6]

J. E. BUSH MEMORIAL HOSPITAL

Little Rock, Arkansas

Established as a corporation on January 23, 1918, by four doctors. The hospital was initially incorporated under the name Booker T. Washington Memorial Hospital. The name was changed to

J. E. Bush Memorial to honor the memory of J. E. Bush. The hospital was a private general hospital with 38 beds in a two story frame building in a residential area. It consisted of one examining room, one operating room, and nursing quarters. By 1925 the hospital increased to 58 beds. The hospital closed in 1927. A nurses training school was affiliated with the hospital. The hospital cared for two societies by contract: the United Friends of America and the Independent Order of Immaculates.[7]

GREAT SOUTHERN FRATERNAL HOSPITAL

Little Rock, Arkansas
Opened November 20, 1919 at 816 West Ninth Street in a two-story, frame building. Seven months later 118 operations had been performed. Both White and Black physicians operated at the hospital. The hospital consisted of 40 beds and a nurse training school from 1921 until 1930.[8]

LENA JORDAN HOSPITAL

Little Rock, Arkansas
Established in 1932 at 1500 Pulaski Street by Lena Jordan, a registered nurse. In the 1930s, the hospital was known as the Arkansas Home and Hospital for Crippled Negro Children. By 1950, the hospital had 20 beds and was equipped for general surgery, medical, and obstetrical care. It was opened to all Black patients regardless of their ability to pay and some White physicians provided services and operated at the hospital.[9]

MOSAIC STATE HOSPITAL

Little Rock, Arkansas
Founded by the Mosaic Templars of America, an international fraternal organization for Blacks, in 1927 (or 1919?) as a 30 bed general hospital.[10]

NEGRO INFIRMARY AND TRAINING SCHOOL (Also known as Little Rock Colored Infirmary)

Little Rock, Arkansas
Opened by Dr. G. W. Hayman on July 8, 1913 in his home at 1701 High Street. The hospitals had eight beds. The purpose of the institution was to care for the Blacks of the entire state. More than 85 major operations were performed in its first year.[11]

ROYAL CIRCLE OF FRIENDS HOSPITAL

Little Rock, Arkansas
A 50-bed general hospital established in 1921 with a nurse training program added in 1927. The hospital was controlled by the fraternal order of the Supreme Royal Circle of Friends of the World.[12]

UNITED FRIENDS OF AMERICA HOSPITAL

Little Rock, Arkansas
Established in 1922 in a house at 714 West Tenth Street. Closed in December 1975. The hospital had 25 beds and a nurse training school from 1924 until 1932. A new hospital built in May 1965 included 25 beds, 36 nursing-home beds, surgical and obstetrical suites, laboratory facilities, x-ray facilities, and other general hospital services. The hospital began to treat White patients in the 1960s.[13]

JULIAN W. ROSS MEDICAL CENTER

Los Angeles, California
Opened in 1957 as a 14-unit medical center with 14 physicians and dentists. Three Black doctors conceived the medical center. An annex was added in 1959. By 1963 the professional staff numbered 28 and the total number employed was over 70. The Medical Center was named after Dr. Julian W. Ross of the Howard University College of Medicine, who had taught several of the physicians while they were students at Howard. The Center was built by Medical Builders of America and financed by Golden State Life Insurance Group. Dr. Earl Claiborne, second highest ranking Black medical officer in the Air Force, agreed to join the medical center upon completion of his

military service.   By 1963 the Center employed about seventy individuals.[14]

ROSE-NETTA HOSPITAL

Los Angeles, California

Founded by Dr. N. Curtiss King in Los Angeles, California in 1941. Contained 17 beds, 6 bassinets, delivery room, diet kitchen, electro-therapy room and two operating rooms. Dr. King received his medical degree from Meharry Medical College in 1924. Also founder and operator of the Dr. N. Curtiss King Hospital (1925-1929) in Newman, California.[15]

FREEDMEN'S HOSPITAL AND ASYLUM
(HOWARD UNIVERSITY HOSPITAL)

Washington, D.C.

Established in 1863 by the federal government at a Civil War military hospital site known as Camp Barker. Dr. Alexander T. Augusta, a major in the U.S. Volunteers, was appointed to head the hospital from 1863 to 1864, the first Black to head a hospital in the United States. From 1881 to the present all surgeon-in-chiefs have been Black. Construction began in 1865 for a new and larger building. A main building and four wings were added in 1908. Additions were completed in later years. The training school for nurses was opened in 1894 and the first ambulance began service. The hospital became identified with Howard University, which was chartered in March 1867.

Throughout its history the hospital has been maintained by federal government: War Department, 1863-1865; Freedmen's Bureau, 1865-1872; Department of Interior, 1872-1939; Federal Security Administration, 1939-1953; and, Department of Health, Education and Welfare, 1953-1965. Since 1965 the hospital has been maintained and authorized by Howard University. Dr. Charles R. Drew and Dr. Paul B. Cornely, noted Black physicians, served as medical directors in 1946-47 and 1947-58, respectively. At several points in the hospital's history, White physicians headed many of the services. From 1871 to 1962 all Howard Medical School graduates (3225) did clinical training at Freedmen's Hospital.

Although rotating internships were available at Freedmen's, it was not until 1936 that the first residency began. In 1938 the hospital had 7,624 inpatients, 8,952 emergencies, and 53,518 clinic visits. Graduate nurse enrollment was 108 and total visiting staff was 100. Total appropriation for the hospital for 1939-1940 was $484,840. The hospital was approved by the American College of Surgeons. It is the oldest institution in the world that provided patient care and physician training to Blacks. In 1941, the hospital had a bed capacity of 406 and was valued at $1,000,000 without equipment. In the same year a tuberculosis annex of 150 beds was added. During fiscal year 1960-61 there were 15,163 inpatients, 3,379 births, and 54,865 outpatient visits.[16]

THE GORDON CONVALESCENT HOME

Washington, D.C.

Founded by Mrs. Ida S. Taylor as a nonprofit and nonsectarian institution for rehabilitation. The home was a 15 room brick structure suitable for 20 patients. It consisted of 9 bedrooms, 4 private, 1 semiprivate, and 4 wards. There were 4 bathrooms, a spacious reception room, dining room, diet kitchen, office room, reading room, upstairs sundeck, front and back verandas, and front and back lawn. The staff consisted of a full-time resident nurse, one 8-hour duty nurse (with others on call), dietitians, male orderly, housekeeper, and house physician (on call).[17]

FAIR HAVEN INFIRMARY

Atlanta, Georgia

Established as a private institution in September 1909 by six Black doctors. The infirmary had a 12 bed capacity and an operating room. The only place in Atlanta where Black surgeons and physicians could hospitalize their patients and treat them. Became the official hospital of the Southern Railway, the Central of Georgia, and the Atlanta Street Railway System.[18]

JACKSON HOSPITAL

Augusta, Georgia
Established in 1852. One of the first U.S. hospitals to care for Black patients. The hospital had no Black staff. It was a three story structure with 50 beds, operating room, and lecture hall. Founded by a group of charitably minded Whites led by Dr. Henry Fraser Campbell of the University of Georgia School of Medicine.[19]

GEORGIA INFIRMARY

Savannah, Georgia
The first hospital in the U.S. founded to provide care to Blacks. Chartered by the Georgia General Assembly on December 24, 1832. Ten thousand dollars was provided to open the hospital through the will of Thomas F. Williams, a Savannah merchant. The hospital was administered and operated by White men for Black patients. Expanded with federal war public works project funds of $101,000, which increased hospital capacity to 89 beds and 16 bassinets.[20]

PROVIDENT HOSPITAL AND NURSES TRAINING SCHOOL

Chicago, Illinois
Established in 1891 at 34th and Dearborn Streets by Black physician Dr. Daniel Hale Williams, a graduate of Northwestern University Medical School in 1883, along with a group of civic and professional leaders. First opened in a two-story frame house with 15 beds. The hospital was founded primarily to provide nursing education for Black women. This was the first Black voluntary hospital in the United States. The staff physicians were both Black and White. In June 1898 the hospital was rebuilt at a new location at 36th and Dearborn Streets with a capacity for 75 patients. In 1917 became the first hospital to offer postgraduate instruction for Black students.

In 1929 the hospital affiliated with the University of Chicago which provided the staff, both physicians and nurses, and instruction and training in various areas. Through a fundraising campaign of $1.3 million spearheaded by the Julius Rosenwald Fund, the hospital opened at 426 East 51st Street. By the late 1930s the hospital facility consisted of a seven story main building with an adjoining four story clinic. Total bed capacity was 144, with 22 bassinets. In 1938 total clinic visits were 111,192, with 41,830 hospital days care for bed patients, 604 major operations, 1,454 minor operations, and 10,995 emergency cases. A 50-year Golden Jubilee Celebration was held January 30, 1941. In 1950 capacity was increased to 206 beds and 35 bassinets as a result of a $750,000 campaign. After 96 years of service the hospital closed in September 1987.[21]

COMMUNITY HOSPITAL

Evanston, Illinois
Established initially as the Evans Sanitorium in 1914 by Dr. Isabelle Garnett, the first Black woman to practice medicine in Evanston. Relocated in 1929 to a two-story brick-veneer, converted private dwelling with 18 beds. The hospital had a drug dispensary, x-ray room, laboratory, operating room, and nurses' dining room. Opened as the New Community Hospital in October 1952 with 54 beds, 12 bassinets, 2 operating rooms, and 2 delivery rooms.[22]

THE EDWARDS MEMORIAL HOSPITAL

Kansas City, Kansas
The Edwards Memorial Hospital for Negroes in Kansas City, Kansas was dedicated on April 18, 1948, as a 105-bed facility. The hospital was named for Walter J. Edwards and Francis Edwards, prominent Blacks in Kansas City.[23]

RED CROSS HOSPITAL

Louisville, Kentucky
Drs. W. T. Merchout and Ellis Whedbee established the hospital in a one-story, four-room frame house in 1899. Moved to a larger two story frame house in 1905. The hospital expanded in size in 1912, 1951, and 1962. A nursing school was a part of the earlier years of the hospital until it was discontinued because of a Kentucky law which forbade the teaching of Whites and Blacks in the same classroom. By the early 1960s the hospital offered three major services: medicine, surgery, and obstetrics. The hospital received accreditation from the Joint Commission on Accreditation of Hospitals

and was a member of the American Hospital Association, the Kentucky Hospital Association, and the Louisville Hospital Council.[24]

FLINT GOODRIDGE HOSPITAL

New Orleans, Louisiana
Opened to the public in 1916 through the merger of Flint Medical College and Sarah Goodridge Hospital. For the first 15 years the hospital was located in a three-story residence. In 1931 a public campaign raised $309,305 to support the construction of the newly merged Flint Goodridge Hospital consisting of a new hospital, nurses' home, and laundry. The four story hospital plant contained a daylight basement, two operating rooms with observation platforms, sterilizing room, delivery room and soundproof nursery, x-ray equipment, pathology laboratory, autopsy room, pharmacy, outpatient department with special treatment and surgical rooms, offices, records room, quarters for interns, kitchen, cafeteria, heating, electrical and refrigerating plants, two elevators, second-floor sun terrace, three 16 bed wards, numerous small wards, and total bed capacity of 100.[25]

PROVIDENT HOSPITAL

Baltimore, Maryland
Started by a few Black physicians on June 13, 1894, in an old private residence with a capacity of 10 beds. The addition of a second house increased the number of beds to 40. In the late 1920s, the hospital had 125 beds consisting of 5 wards and 24 semiprivate rooms. In the year ending September 30, 1929, 1,551 patients were admitted for a total of 25,040 hospital days, 127 births were recorded, and 690 surgical operations performed. A new hospital with 280 beds was built in the late 1960s.[26]

MILLER'S INFIRMARY

Yazoo City, Mississippi
Opened in 1907 by Dr. Lloyd T. Miller, a Black physician. Contained 18 beds.[27]

AFRO-AMERICAN SONS AND DAUGHTERS HOSPITAL

Yazoo City, Mississippi
Opened in 1928 as the first Black owned and operated hospital in Mississippi. Founded by Dr. Lloyd T. Miller and Tom J. Huddleston (businessman). By 1950 had 104 beds and was valued at approximately $100,000.[28]

DOUGLASS HOSPITAL

Kansas City, Missouri
A 45-bed, 12-bassinet institution founded in 1899 by Dr. Solomon H. Thompson and associates and maintained from 1905 by the African Methodist Episcopal Church. The first Black hospital west of the Mississippi.[29]

KANSAS CITY GENERAL HOSPITAL NO. 2

Kansas City, Missouri
Opened for Blacks in 1911. In 1919 had 177 beds after several years of effort by Black physician Dr. Thomas C. Unthank. The hospital was used by Whites until a new hospital was built for Whites, Kansas City General Hospital No. 1. Hospital No. 2 became known as "the Old City Hospital" once it became a Black hospital because it was "35 years old, inadequate, antiquated, dingy, dirty, and unsightly." Renovated at a cost of $87,000. Hospital No. 2 became a training (intern) hospital for Black physicians. In February 1930 reopened as a newly constructed facility at a cost of $300,000 with eight floors and the most modern equipment.[30]

MARTIN LUTHER KING, JR. HOSPITAL

Kansas City, Missouri
Opened in May 1972 as a 100-bed facility. The hospital was a replacement for Wheatley Provident Hospital, a former Black hospital. Funds for the building of the hospital came from donations in the greater Kansas City community by businesses, churches, and over 2,000 individuals and the federal government.[31]

THE PERRY SANITARIUM

Kansas City, Missouri
Opened in 1910 for the purpose of giving to Blacks of Kansas City and vicinity the advantages of first class hospital facilities. At the time it was opened, only one hospital in Kansas City, outside of the general hospital, would admit Black patients. The sanitarium was the result of 14 years of strenuous toil and sacrifice on the part of Dr. J. Edward Perry. Ninety percent of the cases treated during the first year were surgical and some of the most difficult to surgical science. Only three cases out of 108 succumbed after operations. The sanitarium had a capacity of twenty beds. Six nurses were in attendance. The institution received patronage from Missouri, Kansas, and Oklahoma. In 1917 merged with Wheatley-Provident Hospital.[32]

WHEATLEY-PROVIDENT HOSPITAL

Kansas City, Missouri
A private, nonprofit voluntary hospital which served Blacks. It was housed in what was formerly a private school building. Founded by Black physician Dr. John Edward Perry. Began operating as Wheatley-Provident Hospital in 1918. A children department and pediatric center was built in 1923. Initially had 50 beds and 12 bassinets; expanded to 67 beds.[33]

HOMER G. PHILLIPS HOSPITAL

St. Louis, Missouri
Homer G. Phillips Hospital replaced City Hospital #2 as the Black hospital of St. Louis. In 1919 City Hospital #2 opened with a bed capacity of 177. Homer G. Phillips, a local Black attorney, spearheaded efforts to open a more modern facility for Blacks. Homer G. Phillips Hospital opened in 1937 with 728 beds and 49 bassinets, at a cost of $3,160,000. The hospital consisted of five main buildings, service administration, a north and south ward, nurses home, and a training school. A School of Medical Records Library Science, a School for X-Ray Technicians, and intern programs were later added. A new clinic was added costing $1,270,00.[34]

KENNEY MEMORIAL HOSPITAL

Newark, New Jersey

Founded by Dr. John A. Kenney in 1927. The hospital had 30 beds and was valued at $75,000 with equipment in excess of $23,000. In 1934 the hospital was turned over to the Booker T. Washington Hospital Association, representing the Black people of New Jersey, and renamed the Community Hospital. By 1930 the hospital had received 941, patients who spent 14,514 days. Nearly 430 operations had been performed and 83 births occurred. In November, 1929 an outpatients' free clinic was opened with an organized staff of 11 physicians. By 1934, the hospital as a private facility had served 4,543 bed patients, 594 free clinic patients, and conducted 1,109 operations with only 19 deaths.[35]

HARLEM HOSPITAL

New York City

On April 18, 1887, Harlem Hospital opened its doors with a bed capacity of 54. The hospital was established to serve a growing community of Blacks north of Central Park. In 1905 bed capacity was increased to 95. A new hospital opened on April 13, 1907 with a capacity of 150 beds. The average daily patient visits was 154 and by 1910 had increased to 184. Later, after several additions, bed capacity was increased to 1,031 by 1964. The hospital was accredited by the Joint Commission on Accreditation of Hospitals.[36]

VINCENT SANITARIUM AND HOSPITAL

Harlem, New York City

Opened in 1929. Termed the finest private hospital in America owned and staffed by Blacks. Cost was $150,000. Founded by Dr. U. Conrad Vincent, a Black graduate of the Medical School of the University of Pennsylvania and one of the leading urological surgeons in the country. The five-story facility contained a reception room, dental suite, dental laboratory, four room suite for Dr. Vincent, a prescription pharmacy, two-room suite for house physician, superintendent's office, elevator, private and semi-private rooms with baths, four 6-bed wards (total 50 bed capacity), operating room, electric refrigeration and electric call system, diet kitchens, heating plant, and x-ray rooms.[37]

GOOD SAMARITAN HOSPITAL

Charlotte, North Carolina

Established in 1888, under the auspices of the Protestant Episcopal Church, in a brick building with bed capacity of 20 patients. Buildings were later added increasing bed capacity to 65. By 1930 the hospital plant was valued at $159,000. In 1930 existing buildings were remodeled and modernized and a new wing for a nurses' home and outpatient department was added at a cost of $67,000. Had an interracial physician staff. During 1930, the hospital cared for 927 patients, providing 8,641 bed care days at a daily per capita cost of $2.65. Outpatients totaled 284, major surgeries 174, and minor operations 542.[38]

THE LINCOLN HOSPITAL

Durham, North Carolina

Lincoln Hospital of Durham, North Carolina was founded by Dr. A. M. Moore in 1901. The hospital was governed by a 15 member board of trustees (5 Whites and 10 Blacks). The hospital was financed with a gift of $85,550 from Washington Duke, whose name Duke University now carries. Upon opening, Lincoln Hospital served as a 125 bed acute care facility for the Black citizens of Durham and surrounding counties. In 1924 a new hospital was built. Again, the funds primarily responsible for the new hospital were provided by the Duke family. The hospital was approved by the American Medical Association for the training of interns in 1925 and also received accreditation from the Joint Commission. It operated both a nurse anesthetist and a nursing diploma program. In 1929 over 2,300 patients were treated and 295 major and 419 minor surgeries were performed. The hospital had 108 beds and bassinets. A Nurse Training School was recognized by the state. The hospital received a "Class A" rating from the American College of Physicians.[39]

L. RICHARDSON MEMORIAL HOSPITAL

Greensboro, North Carolina

A 12-member board of directors (6 Whites and 6 Blacks) at the urging of several Blacks was formed January 15, 1924 to pursue the hospital project under the name Greensboro Negro Hospital Association. Created from a donation of 4.5 acres of land by a real estate company, $10,000 for equipment from an individual, and $50,000 from another individual, the hospital was formally dedicated on May 27, 1927. In 1927 a 36-month accredited nursing school was established and the first five nurses graduated in 1930. Both Black and White doctors were employed at the hospital. The hospital began with 60 beds, 4 bassinets, 5 graduate nurses, and 1 intern. The hospital was approved by the American Medical Association and the American College of Surgeons. An obstetrical department of 12 beds and 17 bassinets were added in May 1946. By May 1953 the hospital had served a total of 42,000 patients in its first 26 years. The hospital's capacity increased to 96 beds in 1954-55. A new and larger hospital opened May 1966 at a cost of $2.25 million.[40]

LEONARD HOSPITAL

Raleigh, North Carolina

Established in 1888 at a cost of $20,000. The hospital was a three-story brick building with operating room and wards for convalescent surgical patients, lecture room, laboratory, reading room and dissecting room. An additional three story building contained a well equipped chemical laboratory and classrooms. There was also pharmacy building of two stories with classrooms, laboratories, and a dispensary. The hospital cared for up to 80 patients. On February 5, 1912, the hospital became a unit of Leonard Medical School of Shaw University.[41]

ST. AGNES HOSPITAL

Raleigh, North Carolina

Opened October 18, 1896, in an old wooden structure on the grounds of St. Augustine's College, a Protestant Episcopal institution. Dr. Aaron Hunter principal of St. Augustine's School, and Mrs. Sarah Hunter, persuaded the Episcopal Church Women's Auxiliary and Mr.

I. L. Collins of Orange, California to donate $500 and $600, respectively, to the hospital. The first surgery at the hospital was performed on April 6, 1897. The first training school commencement for nurses was held on April 21, 1898, for a class of two graduates. By 1908 the hospital consisted of a three story structure, with five large public wards, six private rooms, and large airy halls on each floor. Capacity was about 60 persons. Cost of plant was about $40,000. Rates were $4.00 per week in public ward; $7.00 to $10.00 in private ward. Senior class of Leonard Medical School attended clinics, operations, and maternity cases. During the year 1921, 1,034 patients were treated at the hospital. In 1928 the hospital was approved for intern training by the American College of Surgeons. In 1930 the hospital was valued at $208,000. By 1941 the hospital was a 100-bed facility. After further years of service, the hospital closed in April 1961.[42]

COMMUNITY HOSPITAL

Wilmington, North Carolina

The Black medical society of Wilmington, North Carolina (with a membership of seven), was the driving force behind the founding of Community Hospital. Donations from Black physicians and the Black community were instrumental in the purchasing a two story frame building. On September 29, 1920 Community Hospital opened with a bed capacity of 20. The key Black physicians on the hospital staff were Drs. Foster Burnett, John Kay, and F. W. Avant. A School of Nursing was opened at the hospital in 1927 and the first class of three nurses graduated in 1930. A second class of four nurses graduated in 1931. At least 254 nurses had graduated from the nursing school by 1964. Dr. Randall C. Roane, a graduate of Howard University School of Medicine, was the first resident physician at Community Hospital in 1938. Dr. Samuel Jones Gray, also a graduate of Howard was the second resident physician. The hospital doubled its bed capacity to 40 in 1939. At the same time, the hospital became jointly owned by the city and the county.[43]

EDWARDS MEMORIAL HOSPITAL

Oklahoma City, Oklahoma
Dedicated on April 18, 1948. A 105-bed, three story modern
institution built at a cost of $431,000.[44]

THE FREDERICK DOUGLASS MEMORIAL
HOSPITAL AND TRAINING SCHOOL

Philadelphia, Pennsylvania
Organized July 1895 and opened on October 31, 1895, by Dr.
Nathan F. Mossell, the first Black physician to graduate from the
University of Pennsylvania Medical School, in a private three story
dwelling at 1512 Lombard Street in Philadelphia. The funds needed
to equipped the hospital were raised by Dr. Mossell and four ladies
auxiliaries. The first fund raising benefit for the hospital was given
February 26, 1896 at the Academy of Music in Philadelphia. The
effort netted $1,600. In 1908 a more modern hospital was built at a
cost of $100,000. The hospital had a staff of Black and White
physicians and served the 50 Black doctors of the city of Philadelphia.
By 1912 the hospital had treated approximately 3,500 inpatients and
40,000 outpatients of all colors. The State of Pennsylvania
appropriated a total of $86,000 for the maintenance of the hospital and
$18,000 for buildings. Black residents raised $77,000 for building and
administration expenses. Expanded in 1919 at a cost of $130,000.
Merged with Mercy Hospital in 1948.[45]

MERCY HOSPITAL

Philadelphia, Pennsylvania
Founded by Blacks in 1907 in a dwelling house at a cost of
$9,900. In 1919 a five-acre lot and a building was purchased at a cost
of $125,000. The hospital had a completely Black staff. Served both
Blacks and Whites. Merged with Douglass Hospital in 1948.[46]

THE HOSPITAL AND TRAINING SCHOOL FOR NURSES

Charleston, South Carolina

The first institution established for the scientific training of Black nurses in Charleston, South Carolina, was opened in 1896. Dr. Alonzo C. McClennan, a Black physician, spearheaded the founding of the hospital. In 1897 the hospital building at 135 Cannon Street was purchased for $4,500. In 1899 an outdoor clinic for babies was established. By 1939 the hospital building included women's and men's medical, surgical, and pediatric wards; private, delivery and operating rooms; and dispensary, sterilizing and X-ray rooms.[47]

WORKING BENEVOLENT SOCIETY HOSPITAL

Greenville, South Carolina

Opened October 10, 1927, with 20 beds and two bassinets. After 2½ years had admitted over 380 patients and performed more than 100 major operations.[48]

HOME INFIRMARY

Clarksville, Tennessee

Established in 1906 by Robert T. Burt, M.D., surgeon-in-chief and sole owner. Cost of building and property was $6,500. The only hospital of its kind in the city, White or Black, making it necessary for the White physicians to send their Black patients there. Both Blacks and Whites contributed linen very liberally, giving sheets, pillow cases, towels, gowns, and the like. The hospital had 32 rooms equipped with modern conveniences.[49]

MERCY HOSPITAL

Memphis, Tennessee

Opened by two Black doctors in 1918 as a 27-bed surgical facility. Operated a school of nursing. As of 1930 more than 3,000 patients had been treated.[50]

MILLIE E. HALE HOSPITAL

Nashville, Tennessee
Founded by Millie E. Hale, wife of prominent Black physician Dr. J.H. Hale, in July 1916. The hospital was the first year-round hospital for Blacks, with 12 beds and 2 nurses in charge. Expanded to 100 beds with four house physicians and Dr. Hale as surgeon-in-chief and 26 nurses.[51]

HOUSTON NEGRO HOSPITAL

Houston, Texas
Opened May 14, 1927, as a 50 bed facility with surgical, obstetrical and medical departments and two operating rooms, clinical and x-ray laboratories, three diet kitchens, main kitchen and dining room. Through its first three years had admitted 1,415 patients. The staff consisted of both Black and White doctors. Became known as Riverside General Hospital.[52]

GOOD SAMARITAN HOSPITAL

San Antonio, Texas
Founded by Rachel Starr (a White) in 1948 as a hospital for the city's 25,000 Blacks. Opened as a 70 bed facility with laboratories, x-ray, fluoroscope and two operating rooms. The first and second floors had six wards and four private rooms.[53]

WHITAKER MEMORIAL HOSPITAL

Newport News, Virginia
In 1908 four physicians pooled their financial resources and temporarily rented a four-room building. This was the birth of Whitaker Memorial Hospital. On May 27, 1914 the charter and articles of incorporation of the hospital were granted and in 1915 the first Black hospital and nurse-training school opened in Newport News, Virginia. The nurse training school before its closure in 1932 graduated 112 nurses. By the early stages of World War II the hospital had increased capacity to 53 beds and 20 bassinets. In December 1944, the hospital was fully accredited by the American College of Surgeons and later by the Joint Commission for the

Accreditation of Hospitals. By 1957 the hospital had admitted 3,496 patients. In 1964 the facility was an 81-bed general hospital with 18 bassinets, with 140 employees.[54]

NORFOLK COMMUNITY HOSPITAL

Norfolk, Virginia
Founded on April 16, 1915, by the Tidewater Colored Hospital Association as the 12 bed Tidewater Hospital. A few years later was named Drake Memorial Hospital. Was renamed Norfolk Community Hospital in 1932 after expansion to a 30 bed facility with the consolidation of a maternity ward established by the Tidewater Colored Graduate Nurses Association. Later expanded to 65 beds in 1939 through a Public Works Act grant. By 1943 had 142 beds, nurses' home, power plant, and garage. The hospital was associated with Howard University College of Medicine, Norfolk State College, and Hampton Institute. The facility received provisional approval from the American College of Surgeons in 1938. In the same year a highly successful outpatient clinic service began, and the hospital began operation of a city beach facility as a supplemental source of revenue (which lasted about 10 years). In 1939 full approval was granted by the American College of Surgeons.[55]

RICHMOND COMMUNITY HOSPITAL

Richmond, Virginia
Richmond Community Hospital was founded in 1902 by a group of 15 physicians and one layman who realized the need for a Black hospital. In 1932, a new facility with 25 beds was built. The hospital was a community-owned nonprofit institution. By 1967 the hospital had a staff of 15, a courtesy staff of 38, and a consulting staff of 12. Included on the courtesy staff were 8 dentists and one podiatrist.[56]

BURRELL MEMORIAL HOSPITAL

Roanoke, Virginia
Burrell Memorial Hospital was founded March 18, 1915 by five physicians and named in honor of Dr. I. D. Burrell. A cottage was bought and remodeled into a 10 bed hospital. The staff included one graduate nurse and three student nurses. In 1921 the hospital was

moved and remodeled at a cost of $25,000. In July 1955 a new 96 bed facility was opened for $1.86 million. The year 1962 was considered the most successful and progressive in the hospital's history. A nursing school was located at the hospital. Several graduates of Howard and Shaw served as volunteer instructors in the nurses' training school. By 1930 a Board of Trustees of 15 members (both White and Black) controlled the institution. The training school was accredited by the Virginia State Board, the American Medical Association, and the American Red Cross. Hospital bed capacity was increased to 55 with three operating rooms, obstetrical delivery room, dental clinic, prenatal clinic, pathologic laboratory, x-ray department, classroom, and hospital and nurses' dormitory. The hospital's property, equipment and grounds were valued at $82,000. In 1955 a new building with 96 beds was constructed at a cost of nearly $2 million. In 1962 the hospital admitted 2,987 patients, provided 23,800 days of patient care, served 940 major and minor surgeries, and employed 130 persons.[57]

NOTES

1. "Cottage Home Infirmary." *Journal of the National Medical Association* 5 (1913): 95.
2. "A Spark, a Flame, a Beacon Light: The Holy Family Hospital." *Journal of the National Medical Association* 55 (1) (January 1963): 86-88.
3. Sister Maria R.S.M., "History of the Saint Martin de Porres Hospital, Mobile, Alabama." *Journal of the National Medical Association* 56 (4) (July 1964): 303-306.
4. Eugene H. Dibble, "The John A. Andrew Memorial Hospital, Tuskegee Institute, Alabama." *Journal of the National Medical Association* 22 (3) (1930): 137-138; Eugene H. Dibble, Louis A. Rabb, and Ruth B. Ballard, "John A. Andrew Memorial Hospital." *Journal of the National Medical Association* 53 (2) (March 1961): 103-118; and "John A. Andrew Memorial Hospital." *Journal of the National Medical Association* 5 (2) (June 1913): 89-92.
5. J. H. Ward, "U.S. Veteran's Hospital." *Journal of the National Medical Association* 22 (3) (1930): 133-134; Albon Lewis Hosley,"The Negro Veterans' Hospital." *The Southern Workman* 55 (1926): 305-314; "The Tuskegee Hospital Muddle." *The Crisis* 26 (5)

(September 1923): 216-218; and Howard W. Kenney and Julian W. Giles, "Tuskegee Veterans Administration Hospital: Present and Future." *Journal of the National Medical Association* 54 (2) (March 1962): 139-145.

6. Edwina Walls, "Some Extinct Black Hospitals of Little Rock and Pulaski County." *Pulaski County Historical Review* 34 (1) (1986): 2-13; and Hugh A. Browne, "A Brief History of McRae Memorial Sanitorium." *Journal of the National Medical Association* 54 (4) (July 1962): 517-518.

7. Ibid., p. 3.

8. Ibid., p. 4.

9. Ibid., p. 8.

10. Ibid., p. 5.

11. Ibid., p. 2.

12. Ibid., p. 6.

13. Ibid., p. 6.

14. Mayo R. DeLilly, "The Julian W. Ross Medical Center." *Journal of the National Medical Association* 55 (4) (July 1963): 261-267.

15. "Rose-Netta Hospital, L.A." *Opportunity* 20 (August 1942): 429.

16. W. Montague Cobb, "A Short History of Freedmen's Hospital." *Journal of the National Medical Association* 54 (3) (May 1962): 271-293; and T. Hold, C. Smith Parker, and R. Terborg-Penn, *A Special Mission: The Story of Freedmen's Hospital, 1862-1962* (Washington, D.C.: Division of Academic Affairs, Howard University, 1975).

17. E. Pauline Myers, "The Gordon Convalescent Home: A Story of Achievement." *National Negro Health News* 16 (July/September 1948): 13-15.

18. "Fair Haven Infirmary." *Journal of the National Medical Association* (1913): 107.

19. W. Montague Cobb, "Integration in Medicine: A National Need." *Journal of the National Medical Association* 49 (January 1957): 1-7.

20. H. Hewes, "Georgia Infirmary. First Hospital in the United States Founded for Negroes." *Negro History Bulletin* (October 1945): 2-23.

21. Henry B. Matthews, "Provident Hospital: Then and Now." *Journal of the National Medical Association* 53 (3) (May 1961): 209-224.

22. "The New Community Hospital of Evanston, Illinois." *Journal of National Medical Association* 45 (1) (January 1953): 74-75.

23. Julia Clarke, "Frances Edwards." *The Crisis* (March 1949): 91.

24. Waverly B. Johnson, "Red Cross Hospital, Louisville, Kentucky." *Journal of the National Medical Association* 57 (4) (July 1965): 332-334.

25. "The History of Flint-Goodridge Hospital of Dillard University." *Journal of the National Medical Association* 61 (6) (November 1969): 533-536; "Sarah Goodridge Hospital." *Journal of the National Medical Association* 5 (2) (June 1913): 94-95; H. W. Knight, "Flint-Goodridge Hospital." *Journal of the National Medical Association* 22 (3) (1930): 130-131; Moise H. Goldstein and B. C. MacLean, "A Hospital That Serves as a Center of Negro Medical Education." *The Modern Hospital* (November 1932): 65-70; and R. B. Eleazer, "Flint Goodridge Hospital." *The Crisis* (July 1933): 151-512.

26. Robert L. Jackson and Emerson C. Walden, "A History of Provident Hospital, Baltimore, Maryland." *Journal of the National Medical Association* 59 (3) (May 1967): 157-165; and R. J. Cross, "Provident Hospital." *Journal of the National Medical Association* 22 (3) (1930): 144-145.

27. "Delta Doctor Performs 34,000 Operations." *Ebony* (March 1950): 27-29.

28. Ibid., p. 28.

29. Cobb, "Integration in Medicine," pp. 3-4.

30. Samuel U. Rodgers, "Kansas City General Hospital No. 2." *Journal of the National Medical Association* 54 (5) (September 1962): 525-544, 639 and; "Three Hospitals." *Journal of the National Medical Association* 22 (3) (1930): 155.

31. "The Martin Luther King, Jr. Hospital of Kansas City, Missouri." *Journal of the National Medical Association* 64 (6) (November 1972): 551-552.

32. John A. Kenney, *The Negro in Medicine* (Tuskegee, Alabama, 1912): 47 and W. Montague Cobb, "John Edward Perry,

M.D." *Journal of the National Medical Association* 48 (1956): 292-296.

33. "Three Hospitals," p. 155.

34. H. Phillip Venable, "The History of Homer G. Phillips Hospital." *Journal of the National Medical Association* 53 (6) (November 1961): 541-555; T. K. Brown, "The Homer G. Phillips Hospital." *The Washington University Medical Alumni Quarterly* 3 (3) (April 1940): 134-138; and James C. McGuire, "Recent Advances at Homer G. Phillips Hospital." *Journal of the National Medical Association* 47 (5) (September 1955): 323-324.

35. John A. Kenney, "Kenney Memorial Hospital." *Journal of the National Medical Association* 22 (3) (1930): 156-157; "Donation of a Hospital to a Community." *The Southern Workman* 64 (May 1953): 154-157; and "Newark All-Negro Hospital Part of Founder's Life Dream." *The Southern Workman* 68 (April 1939): 105-108.

36. Arthur T. Davidson, "A History of Harlem Hospital." *Journal of the National Medical Association* 56 (5) (September 1957): 373-380; "Report on Harlem Hospital." *The Crisis* (March 1934): 83-84; and "Harlem Hospital." *The Crisis* (April 1934): 101-102.

37. William M. Kelley, "The Romance of a Negro Sanatorium in Harlem." *Opportunity* (June 1929): 177-178.

38. Emery L. Rann, "The Good Samaritan Hospital of Charlotte, North Carolina." *Journal of the National Medical Association* 56 (2) (May 1964): 223-226; and Mary Ross, "Improved Negro Facilities Is Hopeful Sign for South." *The Modern Hospital* (October 1932): 53-60.

39. C. D. Watts and F. W. Scott, "Lincoln Hospital of Durham, North Carolina." *Journal of the National Medical Association* 57 (2) (March 1965): 177-183.

40. Wilson O. Elkins, "The History of L. Richardson Memorial Hospital." *Journal of the National Medical Association* 61 (3) (May 1969): 205-212; S. P. Sebastian, "The L. Richardson Memorial Hospital." *Journal of the National Medical Association* 22 (3) (1930): 142-144; Ross, "Improved Negro Facilities Is Hopeful Sign for South," pp. 57-58; and Wilson O. Elkins, "A History of L. Richardson Memorial Hospital." *North Carolina Medical Journal* 30 (April 1969): 146-151.

41. "Leonard Hospital." *Journal of the National Medical Association* 5 (2) (June 1913): 86-89.

42. W. Montague Cobb, "Saint Agnes Hospital, Raleigh, North Carolina, 1896-1961." *Journal of the National Medical Association* 53 (5) (September 1961): 439-446; Lemeul T. Delaney, "St. Agnes Hospital, Raleigh, North Carolina." *Journal of the National Medical Association* 22 (3) (1930): 135-136; and Ross, "Improving Negro Hospital Facilities Is Hopeful Sign for South," pp. 55-57.

43. Hubert A. Eaton, "Community Hospital, Wilmington, North Carolina." *Journal of the National Medical Association* 57 (1) (January 1965): 74-79.

44. "Frances Edwards," p. 91.

45. Edward S. Cooper, "The Mercy-Douglas Hospital." *Journal of the National Medical Association* 53 (1) (January 1961): 1-7; David McBride, *Integrating the City of Medicine: Blacks in Philadelphia Health Care, 1910-1965* (Philadelphia: Temple University Press, 1989), pp. 9-10; Dietrich C. Reitzes, *Negroes and Medicine* (Cambridge: Harvard University Press, 1958), pp. 55-60; "Three Hospitals," p. 155; Elliot M. Rudwick, "A Brief History of Mercy-Douglass Hospital in Philadelphia." *Journal of Negro Education* 20 (1951): 50-66; "The Douglass Hospital of Philadelphia." *The Crisis* 3 (3) (January 1912): 118-120; and John L. Procope, "Mercy-Douglass Hospital Today." *Journal of the National Medical Association* 53 (1) (January 1961): 8-13.

46. Cooper, "The Mercy-Douglas Hospital," pp. 4-5 and Lula G. Warwick, "New Nurses Have a Mercy Hospital and School for Nurses." *Journal of the National Medical Association* 22 (3) (1930): 121; Henry M. Minton, "Mercy Hospital." *Journal of the National Medical Association* 22 (3) (1930): 119-121; Rudwick, "A Brief History of Mercy-Douglass Hospital in Philadelphia," pp. 52-55; and Frances F. Kane, "How Success Was Achieved in Drive for Negro Hospital." *The Modern Hospital* (February 1929): 73-78.

47. "Hospital and Training School for Nurses." *The Hospital Herald* 1 (5) (April 1899): 2.

48. Petra Pinn, "Working Benevolent Society Hospital." *Journal of the National Medical Association* 22 (1930): 147.

49. "The Home Infirmary." *Journal of the National Medical Association* 22 (3) (1930): 162.

50. H. M. Green, "Mercy Hospital Memphis, Tennessee." *Journal of the National Medical Association* 22 (1930): 147.

51. "A Hospital for Negroes with a Social Service Program." *Opportunity* (December 1923): 370.

52. Eugene B. Perry, "Riverside General Hospital." *Journal of the National Medical Association* 57 (3) (May 1965): 258-265; and M. H. Bright, "The Houston Negro Hospital." *Journal of the National Medical Association* 22 (3) (1930): 148.

53. "Better Mousetrap." *Time* (July 26, 1948): 60-61.

54. E. Stanley Grannum, "Whittaker Memorial Hospital." *Journal of the National Medical Association* 56 (2) (March 1964): 119-123 and M. R. Holmes, "Whittaker Memorial Hospital and Training School for Nurses." *Journal of the National Medical Association* 22 (3) (1930): 153.

55. Oswald W. Hoffler, "Norfolk Community Hospital." *Journal of the National Medical Association* 58 (3) (May 1966): 151-155.

56. "The Richmond Community Hospital." *Journal of the National Medical Association* 59 (5) (September 1967): 389-390.

57. William Montague Cobb, "Burrell Memorial Hospital, Roanoke, VA." *Journal of the National Medical Association* 55 (3) (May 1963): 256-257.

4

The Hill-Burton Act
and Black Hospitals

THE HILL-BURTON ACT

The Hospital Survey and Construction Act, commonly known as the Hill-Burton Act, was the federal government's first major intervention in mainstream medical care. The legislation became federal law on August 13, 1946, under the administration of the U.S. Surgeon General with the assistance of the Federal Hospital Council.[1] The purpose of the Hill-Burton Act was to provide federal funds to states for hospital construction, with the intent of building an improved hospital system nationwide.[2] The legislation was a response to the shortage and maldistribution of hospitals and other health facilities recognized by Congress following the Great Depression and World War II. The legislation was passed during President Harry Truman's administration. President Truman asked Congress to pass a five-part comprehensive legislative plan to ensure adequate medical services for all Americans. The Hill-Burton Act was passed as a part of this comprehensive plan.[3] The Surgeon General was charged with administering the regulations and approving applications for funds in the form of grants and loans.

There were two aspects of the legislation, a survey phase and a construction phase. Under the survey phase, the federal government provided assistance in surveying existing institutions in each state and developing of a plan for providing the needed additional facilities. Each state was allotted federal funds to meet one-third of its total expenditures for the surveys. The states also had to maintain a system of licensing that would ensure a minimum standard of facility quality and safety. The second aspect of the legislation, which is the focus of this chapter, provided for federal aid in constructing the needed facilities.

Congress initially appropriated $3 million to assist the states in making surveys and developing plans and $75 million each year for five years to assist in the construction of hospitals and health facilities. State planning required that each state inventory their existing hospital facilities to determine the total number of hospital beds. A survey then determined how many additional beds were needed to meet the needs of all the residents in each state.

The Hill-Burton legislation prescribed the following ratios as the minimum for adequate service in urban areas: for general hospitals, four and a half beds per thousand population; for mental hospitals, five beds per thousand; and for chronic hospitals, two beds per thousand.[4] Ratios were also provided for rural areas. Because complete hospital service could not be located in every rural area and small community, states were required under the Act to plan for general hospitals on an area basis through a coordinated hospital system. Each area would be classified according to the role the general hospital should play in a coordinated hospital system. Public and nonprofit facilities that conformed to the federal and state requirements were eligible for Hill-Burton construction grants. The federal share of a hospital project was limited to one-third of the total costs.

In October 1949 the Hill-Burton Act was amended by Congress, increasing the federal government appropriation to $150 million for the next five years. The legislation also increased the federal government's share for construction to between one-third and two-thirds and established a special priority for beds to be made available to population groups that by race, color, or creed were less adequately served than other groups of the population. However, out of deference to Southern custom the Act contained a "separate but equal" provision that allowed Southern states to build and maintain separate hospital facilities for Blacks or maintain racially separate divisions or wings within one hospital building.

According to Dent, a state met the equitable provision "when the facilities to be built for the group less well provided for heretofore are equal to the proportion of such group in the total population of the area."[5] This did not mean nonsegregation of patients but only an equalization in bed ratios for each state's population group. Under the separate-but-equal provision, 14 states--Alabama, Florida, Georgia, Kentucky, Louisiana, Maryland, Mississippi, Missouri, Oklahoma, North Carolina, South Carolina, Tennessee, Virginia, and West Virginia--planned separate hospital facilities.[6] These states submitted a plan showing the White and other population to be served and the number of hospital beds available to White and other populations.

As a part of their applications, the states were required to submit the following statement: "No person/certain persons (cross out one) in the area will be denied admission to the proposed facilities as patients because of race, creed, or color."[7] If the words, "no person" were crossed out, the State agency was required to indicate on a separate form that, "The requirement of nondiscrimination has been met because this is an area where separate facilities are provided for separate population groups and the State plan otherwise makes equitable provision, on the basis of need, for facilities and services of like quality for each such population group in the area."[8] As a result of these criteria, in North Carolina 31 racially separate facilities received Hill-Burton grants; four were for Blacks.[9]

The Hill-Burton program was continually reauthorized by Congress through 1974. Over its history the program spurred $15.2 billion in project costs, which included about $4.2 billion in grants to about 6,500 hospital projects, about 11,500 total projects, and about 500,000 inpatient beds in nearly 4,000 communities.[10] The program generated about $11.2 billion in non-subsidized construction. About 60 percent of the grants went to private hospitals making the Hill-Burton program a huge subsidy for the hospital industry. About two-thirds of Hill-Burton funds were used for modernization. Table 4.1 shows the amount of Hill-Burton appropriations for each fiscal year from 1948 through 1972.

Interestingly, after the enactment of the Hill-Burton Act, Black physicians, especially those who were members of the National Medical Association, viewed the law with disdain and distrust. The editor of the *Journal of the National Medical Association*, Dr. John A. Kenney, believed that the Black community would not receive an equitable distribution of Hill-Burton funds because of the separate-but-equal clause.[11] There was also the view that Southern states would not provide two-thirds of the construction costs for Black hospitals and that the separate-but-equal clause would continue to maintain a segregated hospital system.[12]

HILL-BURTON AND HOSPITAL SERVICES FOR BLACKS

While it is difficult to determine how many hospitals by the Hill-Burton program provided services and care to Blacks, it is clear that Blacks did benefit to a small extent from the legislation. By April 1, 1949 Dent noted that 218 hospitals had been approved for Hill-Burton construction funds in six Southern states (Mississippi, Alabama, Tennessee, Georgia, Florida, and South Carolina) and Puerto Rico and the Virgin Islands. Of these, four were separate facilities serving Blacks. One each in Montgomery, Mobile, and Birmingham, Alabama and one in Tallahassee, Florida.[13] Further, the total number of hospital beds for Blacks did increase slightly under Hill-Burton, especially in the earlier years of the legislation. Table 4.2 compares the change in the number and percentage of hospital beds between Blacks and Whites from 1946 and 1949 in the states of Alabama, Georgia, and Mississippi. While the number of hospital beds increased in each state for Blacks, the percentage of beds for Blacks in each state was well below their percentage of the population. The percentage of hospital beds for Whites far exceeded their percentage of the population in each of the three states.

McFall also noted increases in the number of acceptable general hospital and mental beds for non-Whites between 1946 and 1950 in two Southern states, Virginia and North Carolina (see Table 4.3). In Virginia the number of acceptable general hospital beds for non-Whites increased from 1,630 to 1,745 and in North Carolina from 1,808 to 2,176.[14] Interestingly, in these two states, the increase in acceptable mental beds for Blacks far exceeded the increase in acceptable general hospital beds for Blacks (see Table 4.3). During this same period in Georgia, the number of generally acceptable beds for Blacks decreased by nearly 400 beds. While in Mississippi, the number of generally acceptable beds for Blacks increased by only 10 beds (see Table 4.4).

Table 4.1
Hill-Burton Appropriations by Fiscal Year, 1948-1972

Fiscal Year	Amount (in thousands)
1948	$75,000
1949	75,000
1950	150,000
1951	85,000
1952	82,500
1953	75,000
1954	65,000
1955	96,000
1956	109,800
1957	123,800
1958	120,000
1959	185,000
1960	185,000
1961	185,000
1962	209,728
1963	220,000
1964	220,000
1965	220,000
1966	258,500
1967	270,000
1968	267,200
1969	267,200
1970	172,200
1971	171,720
1972	194,900

Source: U. S. Department of Health, Education and Welfare, Hill-Burton Program Progress Report, July 1, 1947-June 30, 1971 (Washington, DC: Government Printing Office, 1972), p. 13.

Table 4.2

General Hospital Beds by Race in Alabama, Georgia, and Mississippi, May 1949

State	Population		Existing Beds 1946		Approved Construction		Total Beds		Bed Percentage		Population Percentage	
	White	Colored	White	Colored	White	Colored	White	Colored	White	Colored	White	Colored
Alabama	1,781,462	946,658	3591	1213	939	388	4530	1601	73.89	26.11	65.30	34.70
Georgia	2,058,400	1,069,600	5230	1822	786	161	6016	1983	75.20	24.80	65.81	34.19
Mississippi	1,072,896	1,039,104	2785	1275	997	957	3782	2232	62.88	37.12	50.80	49.20

Source: Albert W. Dent, "Hospital Services and Facilities Available to Negroes in the United States." *Journal of Negro Education* 18 (3) (Summer 1949): 326-322.

Table 4.3

Hospital Facilities by Race in Virginia and North Carolina, 1946 and 1950

	Population	Acceptable General Hospital Beds			Acceptable Mental Hospital Beds		
		1946	1950	# increase	1946	1950	# increase
VIRGINIA							
White	2,015,583	5,240	5,834	(594)	2,388	3,428	(40)
Non-White	622,190	1,630	1,745	(109)	1,460	2,460	(1,000)
NORTH CAROLINA							
White	2,665,750	6,702	8,965	(2,263)	4,220	7,827	(3,607)
Non-White	1,009,250	1,808	2,176	(368)	1,852	2,783	(931)

Source: Compiled from T. Carr McFall, "Needs for Hospital Facilities and Physicians in Thirteen Southern States." *Journal of the National Medical Association* 42 (July 1950): 235-236.

By 1957 Southern states accounted for one-half of 3,514 Hill-Burton projects and by December 31, 1962, Hill-Burton grants had been made to 80 facilities that had been exclusively designated for Whites or Blacks.[15]   Thirteen of these projects were for the use of Blacks at a cost of $4,080,308 million.[16]   The total Hill-Burton contribution to the 80 projects was about $36.8 million. In Atlanta, Georgia, a wing for Blacks known as the Hughes Spalding Pavilion was added to Grady Memorial Hospital at a cost of $1.85 million. About 60 percent of the funds came from the Hill-Burton Act.[17] The Spalding Pavilion was a five-story air-conditioned hospital with 116 beds, 35 bassinets, kitchen, laundry, and morgue.[18]

In Georgia the Hill-Burton program was inaugurated in 1947. By September 1, 1952 twenty-nine new hospitals in Georgia had been opened with Hill-Burton Funds. A study focusing on 17 of the hospitals that had been in operation one year or more indicated that they served Black patients.[19] However, the hospitals did not cl early indicate whether Black patients were served on a segregated or integrated basis. In Atlanta, by the early 1960s, of 4,000 available beds only 680 were available to Blacks, including 430 at the Spalding Pavilion of Grady Memorial.[20] In other words, the one-third of the population in Atlanta that is Black, had available to them one-sixteenth of the hospital beds.[21]

In North Carolina, the Hill-Burton program built more racially separate hospital facilities than in any other state. Under the separate-but-equal provision of the North Carolina plan, 31 racially separate hospital facilities received grants; four were for Black facilities.[22] In North Carolina, as in Georgia, the state Hill-Burton Agency reported to the U.S. Surgeon General that the total number of beds in each reporting area of the state was found to be proportionately equal to the division of the population by race. However, the U.S. Public Health Service, which the Surgeon General administered, did not determine the extent to which this proportional equality was in fact provided.[23]

BLACK HOSPITALS RECEIVING HILL-BURTON FUNDS

Through a comparison of the *Hill-Burton Register* for the years 1947-1972 with the list of Black hospitals compiled in Appendix I. A small number of Black hospitals can be discerned as recipients of Hill-Burton funds. Table 4.5 shows the state location and name of the facility, type of construction, beds provided, estimated total cost, federal cost and the date the project was initially approved. Although Table 4.5 is not a complete listing of Black hospitals receiving Hill-Burton funds, it does provide a picture of how federal policy assisted in a very small way in the construction and modernization of Black hospitals. Most of the Hill-Burton funds were used for addition and addition and remodeling of Black hospitals. It seems only a few Black hospitals were constructed as new with Hill-Burton funds. Martin DePorres Hospital (Mobile, Alabama), Florida A & M Hospital (Tallahassee, Florida), Lincoln County Hospital (Fayetteville, Tennessee) and Harlem Hospital (New York City) were among the first Black hospitals to receive Hill-Burton funds. About 4,400 new beds were added to Black hospitals. Table 4.5 shows that approximately $33 million or some one percent of Hill-Burton funds were expended on Black hospitals. Table 4.5 also shows that some 38 separate hospital projects involving Black hospitals, or White hospitals with Black wards, received Hill-Burton funds. Several of these hospitals received multiple Hill-Burton grants.

However, one problem that the Hill-Burton Act did not address was "the exclusion of Negro professional and technical personnel from hospitals which are not exclusively devoted to Negro patients."[24] The legislation specified that the federal government shall have no control over the personnel in hospitals built with federal funds. The implementation of the Hill-Burton Act was a state responsibility and the state controlled the personnel and the newly constructed hospital or hospital addition.

THE BLACK COMMUNITY'S RESPONSE TO HOSPITAL SEGREGATION AND THE HILL-BURTON ACT

As a response to the continuing problem of hospital segregation, the first Imhotep National Conference on Hospital Integration was held March 8-9, 1957, in Washington, D.C., eleven years after the Hill-Burton Act. The Conference was sponsored by the National Medical Association, the Medico-Chirurgical Society of the District of

Table 4.4
Hospital Beds by Race in Georgia and
Mississippi, 1946 and 1950

	Population	Acceptable General Hospital Beds			Acceptable Mental Hospital Beds		
		1946	1950	Number Increase	1946	1950	Number Increase
GEORGIA							
White	2,142,000	5,044	5,502	488	6,356	6,332	-24
NonWhite	1,083,000	1,862	1,493	-369	2,995	2,995	0
MISSISSIPPI							
White	1,077,468	3,409	3,439	30	2,842	2,937	95
Nonwhite	1,043,532	1,710	1,720	10	1,039	1,665	626

Source: Compiled from T. Carr McFall, "Needs for Hospital Facilities and Physicians in Thirteen States."
Journal of the National Medical Association 42 (July 1950): 235-236.

Table 4.5
Hill-Burton Funds to Black Hospitals

| Location | Name of Facility | Type of Construction | Beds Provided | Initial Estimated Cost | | Approval |
				Total	Federal	
ALABAMA						
Ensley	Holy Family Hospital	(1)	62	$ 924,404	$ 597,874	7/52
Mobile	Martin DePorres Hospital	(1)	35	$ 611,425	$ 195,475	4/48
Mobile	Martin DePorres Hospital	(5)	22	$ 704,648	$ 300,000	5/65
Selma	Good Samaritan Hospital	(4)	24	$ 142,325	$ 94,883	2/56
Selma	Good Samaritan Hospital	(6)LTC	69	$1,135,426	$ 664,000	10/62
Tuskegee	John A. Andrews Memorial Hospital	(8)	105	$3,898,653	$1,000,000	11/66
Tuskegee	John A. Andrews Memorial Hospital	(5)		$ 637,671	$ 309,000	3/67

Table 4.5 Continued

CALIFORNIA					
Los Angeles	Martin Luther King Jr., Hospital	(1)	394	$27,394,400 $4,212,042	9/67
DISTRICT OF COLUMBIA					
Washington	General Hospital	(6)	128	$2,432,909 $ 525,914	6/49
Washington	General Hospital	(2)		$ 7,800 $ 2,600	1/53
Washington	General Hospital	(3)	180	$1,316,452 $ 395,500	1/61
FLORIDA					
Jacksonville	Brewster Hospital	(2)LTC	44	$ 262,487 $ 129,752	4/57
Jacksonville	Brewster Hospital	(2)	32	$ 786,794 $ 340,000	2/59
Tallahassee	Florida A&M Hospital	(1)	116	$1,923,119 $ 641,040	3/48
West Palm Beach	Pine Ridge Hospital	(2)LTC	30	$ 829,108 $ 90,000	2/57
GEORGIA					
Atlanta	Hughes Spalding Hospital	(2)	116	$1,725,984 $1,035,590	9/49

84

ILLINOIS						
Chicago	Provident Hospital	(5)	30	$ 527,000	$ 204,476	6/49
Chicago	Provident Hospital	(2)		$ 285,000	$ 62,333	9/57
INDIANA						
Indianapolis	Community Hospital	(2)LTC	50	$ 649,699	$ 142,576	5/62
Indianapolis	Community Hospital	(2)	62	$1,529,112	$ 498,747	6/69
Indianapolis	Community Hospital	(2)LTC	158	$5,244,156	$ 461,061	6/69
Indianapolis	Community Hospital	(2)		$1,002,432	$ 322,011	5/62
Indianapolis	Community Hospital	(2)	168	$2,925,984	$ 565,016	5/62
Indianapolis	Community Hospital	(2)		$ 808,868	$ 209,585	6/69
KENTUCKY						
Louisville	Kings Daughter Home		94	$1,241,596	$ 794,621	5/65
LOUISIANA						
New Orleans	Charity Hospital	(2)		$ 488,099	$ 313,342	12/49

85

Table 4.5 Continued

New Orleans	Charity Hospital	(5)	153	$ 510,800	$ 292,500	4/50
New Orleans	Flint-Goodridge Hospital	(5)	136	$1,239,432	$ 680,716	10/58
MARYLAND						
Baltimore	Provident Hospital	(2)	12	$ 209,514	$ 52,074	11/52
Baltimore	Provident Hospital	(4)		$1,308,930	$ 233,939	8/67
Baltimore	Provident Hospital	(4)	122	$3,618,257	$ 625,000	8/67
MICHIGAN						
Highland Park	Highland Park General Hospital	(2)		$ 127,245	$ 50,768	6/56
Detroit	SW Detroit Hospital	(4)		$1,821,410	$ 300,000	6/71
Detroit	SW Detroit Hospital	(4)	247	$14,437,490	$ 980,980	6/71
MISSOURI						
St. Louis	Homer G. Phillips Hosp.			$ 973,080	$ 165,111	2/60
Kansas City	MLK Memorial Hospital	(4)	54	$3,421,022	$1,000,000	7/68

NEW YORK						
New York City (Brooklyn)	Kings County Hospital	(3)		$ 89,327	$ 29,776	11/48
New York City	Harlem Hospital	(3)		$ 30,823	$ 10,274	11/48
NORTH CAROLINA						
Henderson	Jubilee Hospital	(1)	30	$ 405,148	$ 196,479	8/57
Greensboro	L. Richardson Memorial Hospital	(5)	8	$ 156,630	$ 77,000	8/57
Durham	L. Richardson Memorial Hospital	(4)	185	$2,711,589	$1,485,000	4/63
Raleigh	St. Agnes Hospital	(4)		$ 86,356	$ 36,924	2/50
OHIO						
Cleveland	Cuyahoga County Hospital	(2)		$ 218,730	$ 72,910	6/58

87

Table 4.5 Continued

SOUTH CAROLINA				
Columbia	Good Samaritan Waverly Hospital	(1)	$ 223,668 $ 131,312	6/50
Charleston	McClendon Banks Memorial Hospital	(1)	30	$ 705,609 $ 352,730	1/56
TENNESSEE				
Memphis	E. H. Crump Memorial Hospital	(1)	128	$2,473,262 $ 848,000	6/53
Memphis	City of Memphis Hospital	(2)	147	$7,269,195 $2,064,920	12/62
Fayetteville	Lincoln County Hospital	(2)	35	$ 497,409 $ 164,750	6/48
Fayetteville	Lincoln County Hospital	(9)	46	$1,072,987 $ 553,498	8/66
Nashville	Hubbard Hospital	(5)	115	$1,710,545 $ 872,274	2/62
Nashville	Riverside Sanitarium Hosp.	(4)	50	$2,913,327 $ 811,500	3/70

88

Table 4.5 Continued

VIRGINIA						
Hampton	Dixie Hospital	(1)	185	$4,268,353	$1,653,763	4/56
Hampton	Dixie Hospital	(5)	64	$ 952,362	$ 513,645	3/64
Newport News	Whittaker Memorial Hosp.	(2)	30	$ 715,930	$ 345,000	4/55
Newport News	Whittaker Memorial Hosp.	(5)	39	$ 867,936	$ 476,047	1/64
Norfolk	Norfolk Community Hosp.	(5)		$ 418,516	$ 227,948	5/64
Norfolk	Norfolk Community Hosp.	(5)	94	$ 892,844	$ 477,620	5/64
Richmond	Richmond Memorial Hosp.	(1)	411	$5,101,732	$1,650,409	11/52
Richmond	Richmond Memorial Hosp.	(7)	50	$1,447,699	$ 779,900	5/63
Richmond	Richmond Memorial Hosp.	(2)		$ 108,618	$ 53,696	5/63
Roanoke	Burrell Memorial Hosp.	(1)	80	$1,645,847	$ 539,972	11/52

Source: Derived from U.S. Department of Health Education and Welfare (Public Health Service), Hill-Burton Project Register 1947-69-71 (Washington, DC: U.S. Government Printing Office, 1969, 1971, 1972).
(1) New; (2) Addition; (3) Remodeling; (4) Replacement; (5) Addition and Remodeling; (6) Addition and Replacement; (7) Addition, Remodeling, and Replacement; (8) Remodeling and Replacement; (9) Partial Replacement.
TLC = Long Term Care Unit.

89

Columbia, and the National Association for the Advancement of Colored People (NAACP). The stated purposes of the Conference included the following:

> To bring together representatives of all interests among hospitals, the public, the healing professions, and government agencies, which are concerned with this problem.
> To provide a complete, comprehensive situation through-out the country as it exists today through first-hand presentations from various regions.[25]

Imhotep was chosen as the conference name for two reasons: "First, as a reminder that a dark skin was associated with distinction in medicine before that of any other color, this served to emphasize the dignity of the approach to the problem. Second, because the name meant, 'He Who Cometh in Peace,' the sponsoring organization came in peace in a time of emotional tension."[26]

The Conference was attended by 200 delegates from 21 states representing 16 constituent societies of the National Medical Association, the NAACP, and four branches of the National Urban League and various medical and hospital societies. The Conference was primarily devoted to identifying the various forms of hospital discrimination and acquainting the attendees with the forms of discrimination.

Dr. W. Montague Cobb, who was chairman of the NAACP National Health Committe, a member of the Board of Directors, and longtime Editor of the *Journal of the National Medical Association*, served as chairman of the Conference. One of the Conference's first actions was to vote unanimously to seek an amendment to the Hill-Burton Act deleting provisions for racial segregation.[27] The Conference also voted unanimously to work "continuously and vigorously, in the spirit of amity" until "racial discrimination has been eliminated from all hospitals in the United States."[28] Prominent speakers at the Conference included Representative Barratt O'Hara (Illinois), Congresswoman Florence P. Dwyer (New Jersey), Roy

Wilkins (NAACP Executive Secretary), Dr. Robert S. Jason (Dean, Howard University College of Medicine), Dr. T. R. M. Howard (President, National Medical Association), and Dr. Edward C. Mazique (President, Medico-Chirurgical Society).[29] Also in attendance at the Conference was Robert M. Cunningham, editor of the widely read periodical *The Modern Hospital*.[30] Cunningham gave visibility to the Conference by writing an article about it in the April 1957 issue of his publication and by discussing the Conference as keynote speaker at the 1957 meeting of the Southeastern Hospital Conference in Atlanta, Georgia.[31] Cunningham had urged an end to hospital discrimination as early as 1951.[32] His support for hospital integration was most important because *Modern Hospital* was a major publication in the hospital industry.

The second Conference was held in Chicago on May 23-24, 1958. This meeting focused on techniques used against hospital discrimination in one major city.[33] The third conference, held in Washington, D.C., on May 22-23, 1959, focused on means of dealing with hospital segregation and the attitudes of White professional personnel.[34] At the 1962 Conference, held May 25-26, 1962, in Washington, D.C., President Kennedy sent a special letter of greeting to the attendees advising them that the U.S. Attorney General had intervened in a federal court case to support the argument that the segregation clause (separate-but-equal provision) in the Hill-Burton Act was unconstitutional. Senator Jacobs K. Javits (R-NY), a supporter of hospital integration, was a prominent speaker at the Conference, along with Attorney Jack Greenberg who was Chief Counsel of the NAACP Legal Defense and Educational Fund.[35] The sixth and final Conference was held in 1963 in Atlanta, Georgia. The Imhotep Conference was discontinued after the passage of the Civil Rights Act of 1964. President Kennedy also sent a letter to the 1963 conference pointing out that the efforts of the Imhotep Conference were "perfectly in tune with that of the federal government."[36]

For each conference invitations were sent to those organizations representing the predominantly White professional and hospital power structure, asking them to send representatives. It would seem that Conference leaders believed that having official representation from

the White professional and hospital power structures in attendance
would bring an end to hospital segregation. These organizations,
however, sent only observers (not high-ranking officials) or no one at
all. The American Hospital Association, the American Medical
Association had observers in attendance at the first conference. Other
organizations in attendance were the U.S. Public Health Service, the
National Health Council, the National Association of Social Workers,
the District of Columbia Hill-Burton Advisory Council, the University
of Pittsburgh, the Physicians Forum, National AFL-CIO, Hampton
Institute, and others including a number of hospital representatives.
The American Medical Association sent an observer to the 1959
conference. The American Nurses Association sent observers to the
1957 and 1963 conferences.[37]

Ironically, when the U.S. Department of Health, Education, and
Welfare convened a Conference on the Elimination of Hospital
Discrimination in July 1964 (supported by President Lyndon Johnson)
all the organizations that did not officially attend the Imhotep
Conferences were well represented. This included such organizations
as the Federal Hospital Council, the American Hospital Association,
the American Medical Association, the American Dental Association,
and the American Nurses Association. The National Medical
Association and the National Dental Association (both Black
organizations) were represented at the Conference.[38]

At the 1964 conference, to the dismay of the attendees who were
expecting an appearance by President Johnson, Associate Special
Counsel to the President Hobart Taylor (a Black), represented the
President and urged all those in attendance to support what would be
explained to them. Taylor's appearance, perhaps more than his
words, was in itself a powerful message to the assembled hospital
power structure of the country. Department of Health, Education and
Welfare (DHEW) Secretary Anthony J. Celebrezze said that President
Johnson expected hospitals to comply with the Civil Rights Act of
1964 and compliance would avoid needless controversy and litigation.
This 1964 DHEW Conference was termed the Eighth Imhotep
Conference by Dr. W. Montague Cobb who conceived and organized
the first Imhotep Conference.[39]

THE JUDICIAL CHALLENGE TO HILL-BURTON

Until 1964 the Black hospital was the primary source of hospital care for the Black community. In the early 1960s in Atlanta, only 630 of 4,500 hospital beds were available to Blacks, who comprised 50 percent of the population.[40] In Birmingham, Alabama, where Blacks were 40 percent of the population, only 574 of 1,762 hospital beds were allocated to Blacks. In 1959 in Baltimore, only 7 of 17 hospitals offered accommodations to Blacks.[41] By 1963 70 segregated hospital facilities had received Hill-Burton funding, and many others, while not segregated, engaged in various overt and covert discriminatory practices.[42]

In the early 1960s medical civil rights activists and hospital integration proponents began to launch a political and legal attack on hospital segregation. In Congress on September 23, 1961, Senator Jacob Javits (R-NY) introduced Senate Bill 2625 to amend the Hill-Burton Act to prohibit discrimination in any respect whatsoever on account of race, creed, or color in hospital facilities.[43] Senator Javits argued that "nothing could be more pernicious than racial discrimination and segregation in the medical field." The bill was tabled by a vote of 37 to 33.[44] In the 88th Congress Senator Javits reintroduced a similar bill with support from the American Hospital Association, the American Public Health Association, and the Catholic Hospital Association, who had passed resolutions calling for the elimination of the separate-but-equal clause.[45] On the legal front, a major hospital case was about to unfold.

Simkins v. Moses H. Cone Memorial Hospital

On February 12, 1962, 11 Black citizens, six physicians, three dentists, and two patients, of Greensboro, North Carolina, filed suit against Moses H. Cone Memorial Hospital and the Wesley Long Community Hospital. Both hospitals had received Hill-Burton funds. Cone Hospital received $1,276,950 (grants in 1954 and 1960) and Long Hospital $1,708,150 (grants in 1954 and 1961) (see Table 5.1).[46] For Cone Memorial the grants represented approximately 15 percent of the total combined construction costs. For Long Community the grants represented about 50 percent of the combined total construction costs.[47] Cone Memorial had a policy of denying staff privileges to Black practitioners and admitted Blacks only under limited circumstances. Long Community also denied privileges to Black practitioners and admitted no Black patients. The suit represented the first litigation challenging the constitutionality of the Hill-Burton Act antidiscrimination clause. Three attorneys from the NAACP Legal Defense and Educational Fund including, Chief Counsel Jack Greenberg, represented the plaintiffs, along with an attorney from Durham, North Carolina.[48]

The suit charged that the exclusion of Black physicians and dentists from the staff of hospitals, the denial of admission of Black patients, and the separate but equal antidiscrimination clause of the Hill-Burton Act were in violation of the Fourteenth and Fifth amendments of the Constitution. The U.S. District Court disagreed with the plaintiffs on the grounds that private hospitals were not instrumentalities of the states or the federal government. Upon appeal, the Fourth Circuit reversed on the rationale that receipt of Hill-Burton funds represented the "necessary" degree of federal and state involvement and participation. The Supreme Court allowed the decision to stand.[49] The American Public Health Association and the U.S. Department of Justice filed briefs supporting the plaintiffs.

The Department of Health, Education, and Welfare published new regulations on May 19, 1964 in the *Federal Register* in response to the *Simkins* ruling. The new regulations stated: "Before a construction application is recommended by a State agency for approval, the State agency shall obtain assurance from the applicant that all portions and services of the *entire* facility for construction of which, or in connection with which, aid under the Federal Act is sought, *will be made available without discrimination on account of race, creed, or color; and that no professional qualified person will be discriminated against on account of race, creed, or color with respect to the privilege of professional practice in the facility*"[50] (emphasis added).

THE U.S. COMMISSION ON CIVIL RIGHTS, RACE BIAS, AND HILL-BURTON

In 1963 the U.S. Commission on Civil Rights published its findings on race bias in hospitals.[51] The report was based on public hearings, staff field studies, reports of state of civil rights advisory boards, and a mail survey of 398 hospitals in 34 states; on a regional basis, 130 hospitals surveyed were in Southern states. The remaining hospitals surveyed were in other regions. About 55 percent or 219 hospitals responded to the survey. About 64 hospitals responded from Southern states. The Commission found that 60 hospitals had policies of exclusion or segregation. About 59 of the 60 hospitals were licensed by a political subdivision, 45 were incorporated under state law, 20 hospitals were built or remodeled with federal, state or local government funds, and 36 hospitals received Hill-Burton grants, with 3 obtaining funds under the separate-but-equal provision. The other 33 hospitals, located in 14 Southern and border states, practiced separate living accommodations.[52]

In some specific cities, the Commission found the following. In Memphis, Tennessee, a 128 bed city-owned hospital built partially with Hill-Burton funds was the only general accredited facility available to Black paying patients. Three large private church related facilities with a total of 2,082 beds did not admit Blacks. Other small facilities including a Black hospital did admit Black patients.[53] In Nashville, the only hospital facility available to Blacks was Hubbard Hospital (a Black hospital)-at the time a 30 bed facility. No Blacks were admitted to the other four general hospitals (two church related) in the city. One other hospital built partially with a $2 million Hill-Burton grant maintained separate ward facilities for Black adults. In the local city-county hospital, which received both local public and Hill-Burton funds a wing of 28 beds was reserved for Black patients.[54]

In Charleston, South Carolina, where six hospitals were located (one church related), only one, a county owned facility, was available to Black patients and Black physicians. The city was about 36 percent Black. One of the segregated facilities was a recipient of Hill-Burton funds, and another facility built largely with Hill-Burton funds admitted Blacks on a segregated basis.[55] In Kansas City, Kansas, of

five general hospitals one was used exclusively by Blacks. The Black
hospital was the only one for which Hill-Burton funds were not used.
Three hospitals admitted Blacks to separate rooms.[56] In Greensboro,
North Carolina, two government-owned hospitals providing services
to Whites only were recipients of Hill-Burton funds.[57]

The Commission also reported that from 1946 to 1963, 89 Hill-
Burton grants totaling nearly $40 million were provided to finance
construction or remodeling of separate hospital facilities for Whites
and Blacks. About 10 percent or $4 million supported facilities for
Blacks.[58] Overall, by 1963 the Hill-Burton program was the largest
investor in hospitals of all kinds, and the program practically rebuilt
the hospital system nationwide. By 1963 the Hill-Burton program was
responsible for more than "700,000 general beds, about 500,000 long
term beds, 6810 hospital and health centers, 500,000 beds for mental
patients and about 64,000 for patients with tuberculosis."[59] Over the
13-year period between 1948-1961, $1.6 billion in Hill-Burton funds
were expended. Max Seham characterized the Hill-Burton program
as "a Dr. Jekyll to 'Whites' and a cruel Mr. Hyde to the Negroes."[60]

NOTES

1. Title VI of the Public Health Service Act of August 13, 1946,
Public Law Number 79-725, Sections 601, 60 Statute 1041. The
Federal Hospital Council was composed of 8 members appointed by
the Federal Security Administrator. The one Black member, Dr.
Albert W. Dent--President of Dillard University and Director of the
University Flint Goodridge Hospital--headed the Council's Advisory
Committee on Nondiscrimination.

2. The Hill-Burton Act amended the Public Health Service Act of
July 1, 1944.

3. See C. B. Chapman and J. M. Talmadge, "Historical and
Political Background of Federal Health Care Legislation." *Law and
Contemporary Problems* 35 (2) (Spring 1970): 334-347; and P.A.
Brandon, "The Right of Access of the Medically Underserved to
Health Care Services." *Journal of Legal Medicine* 2 (3) (September
1981): 297-345; 329, notes 113-119.

4. Van M. Hoge, "The National Hospital Construction Program." *Journal of the National Medical Association* 40 (3) (May 1948): 102-106.

5. Albert W. Dent, "Hospital Services and Facilities Available to Negroes in the United States." *Journal of Negro Education* (1949): 331.

6. U.S. Commission on Civil Rights, *Report of the U.S. Commission on Civil Rights, 1963* (Washington, DC: Government Printing Office): 130.

7. Ibid., p. 130.

8. Ibid., p.131.

9. Ibid., p. 132.

10. D. Feshbach, "What's Inside the Black Box: A Case Study of Allocative Politics in the Hill-Burton Program." *International Journal of Health Services* 9 (2) (1979): 313-339.

11. John A. Kenney, "Federal Versus State Control." *Journal of the National Medical Association* 38 (1946): 74.

12. See "Medical Legislation." *Journal of the National Medical Association* 39 (1947): 175.

13. Dent, "Hospital Services and Facilities Available to Negroes in the United States," p. 331.

14. T. C. McFall, "Needs for Hospital Facilities and Physicians in Thirteen Southern States." *Journal of the National Medical Association* 42 (2) (July 1950): 235-236.

15. Editorial, *American Journal of Public Health* (1957): 1447; and U.S. Commission on Civil Rights, *Report of the U.S. Commission on Civil Rights, 1963*, p. 131.

16. U.S. Commission on Civil Rights, *Report of the U.S. Commission on Civil Rights, 1963*, p. 131.

17. "For Negroes Only." *Time* (June 30, 1952): 64. For a detailed discussion of the events and activities that led to the building of the Hughes Spalding Pavilion and subsequent problems see Dietrich C. Reitzes, *Negroes and Medicine* (Cambridge, MA: Harvard University Press, 1958), pp. 280-290.

18. "For Negroes Only," p. 64. Grady Memorial Hospital later received Hill-Burton funds of $462,000 for the construction of a Black

nurses' residence, $13,200 for a psychiatric addition, and $278,929 for a diagnostic and treatment center. See "Texts of the Atlanta and Butner, N.C. Suits." *Journal of the National Medical Association* 55 (1) (January 1963): 51.

19. R. C. Williams, "One Year of Operating Experiences of 17 Hospitals Built under Hill-Burton." *Journal of the Medical Association of Georgia* (December 1952).

20. *Journal of the National Medical Association*, 1962: 257.

21. Ibid.

22. U.S. Commission on Civil Rights, *Report of the U.S. Commission on Civil Rights*, 1963, p. 132.

23. Ibid.

24. Hoge, "The National Hospital Construction Program," p. 104.

25. "The Black American in Medicine." *The Journal of the National Medical Association* (Supplement) (December 1981): 1197.

26. Ibid.

27. "Along the N.A.A.C.P. Battlefront." *The Crisis* (April 1957): 219-220.

28. Ibid., p. 219.

29. Ibid.

30. "Hospital Discrimination and the Sixth Imhotep Conference." *Journal of the National Medical Association* 54 (1) (March 1962): 253-255.

31. Robert M. Cunningham, "National Conference Seeks Acceptance of Negro Doctors and Patients in Hospitals." *The Modern Hospital* 88 (4) (April 1957).

32. Robert M. Cunningham, "Are Hospitals for the Sick--Or Just Some of the Sick." *Modern Hospital* 76 (June 1951): 51.

33. "Third Imhotep Conference." *The Crisis* (June/July 1959): 351-352.

34. Ibid., p. 352.

35. "The Black American in Medicine," p. 1198 and "Notables to Address Sixth Imhotep Conference." *Journal of the National Medical Association* 54 (2) (March 1962): 256.

36. Ibid., p. 1198.

37. Ibid., pp. 1197-1198.

38. Ibid., pp. 1197-1198.

39. Ibid., pp. 1197-1198.

40. Max Seham, "Discrimination against Negroes in Hospitals." *The New England Journal of Medicine* 271 (18) (October 29, 1964): 940-942

41. Ibid., p. 941.

42. K. Wing and M. Rose, "Health Facilities and the Enforcement of Civil Rights." In Ruth Roemer and George McKray (eds.), *Legal Aspects of Health Policy: Issues and Trends* (Westport, CT: Greenwood Press, 1980).

43. "Hospital Discrimination and the Sixth Imhotep Conference," p. 254.

44. Seham, "Discrimination against Negroes in Hospitals," p. 942.

45. Ibid., p. 942.

46. "Greensboro, North Carolina Group Files Historic Suit Against Hospital Exclusion." *Journal of the National Medical Association* 54 (2) (March 1962): 259.

47. K. Wing, "Title VI and Health Facilities: Forms without Substance." *Hastings Law Journal* 30 (1) (September 1978): 137-190.

48. "Greensboro, North Carolina Group Files Historic Suit against Hospital Exclusion," p. 259. This case has been referred to as "the 'grandaddy of hospital desegregation suits' for it did what [B]lack medical reformers had been unable to do for fifteen years: eliminate segregation from hospitals funded by the Hill-Burton Act." See Edward H. Beardsley, "Good-bye to Jim Crow." *Bulletin of the History of Medicine* 60 (1986): 378.

49. See *Simkins v. Moses H. Cone Memorial Hospital*, 211 F. Supp. 628 (M.D.N.C. 1962); 323 F. 2d. 959 (4th Cir. 1963); cert. denied 376. U.S. 938 (1964).

50. See U.S. Commission on Civil Rights, *Equal Opportunity in Hospitals and Health Facilities: Civil Rights Under the Hill-Burton Program* (Washington, D.C.: U.S. Government Printing Office, 1965). See also K. Wing and M. Rose, "Health Facilities and the Enforcement of Civil Rights." In Ruth Roemer and G. McKray (eds.) *Legal Aspects of Health Policy: Issues and Trends* (Westport, CT: Greenwood Press, 1980).

51. U.S. Commission on Civil Rights, *Report of the U.S. Commission on Civil Rights,* (Washington, D.C.:   Government Printing Office, 1963.

52. Ibid., pp. 134-136.

53. Ibid., pp. 137.

54. Ibid., pp. 139.

55. Ibid., pp. 140.

56. Ibid., pp. 140.

57. Ibid., pp. 133.

58. Ibid., pp. 141-142.

59. Seham, "Discrimination against Negroes in Hospitals," p. 942.

60. Ibid.

5

The Decline of the Black Hospital and Contemporary Public Policy

Nathaniel Wesley, Jr., a noted observer of Black hospitals, identified about 32 Black hospitals around the United States in 1984,[1] a decrease from 40 in 1983. Seven of the hospitals closed or discontinued inpatient services in 1983. A number of these hospitals became privately managed or owned by private, for-profit hospital chains or nonprofit entities. For example, Fairview Medical Center (Montgomery, Alabama), Martland Hospital (Newark, New Jersey), Richmond Community Hospital (Richmond, Virginia) and Whittaker Memorial Hospital (Newport News, Virginia) became privately managed by the Hospital Corporation of America, a private, for-profit hospital chain. Detroit Receiving Hospital (Detroit, Michigan), L. Richardson Memorial Hospital (Greensboro, North Carolina) and Memphis Regional Medical Center (Memphis, Tennessee) became privately managed by nonprofit organizations.[2]

According to Wesley, over the 17 year period from 1961 to 1988, 71 Black hospitals either closed, merged, converted, or consolidated. The most common action was closure. Forty-nine of these hospitals actually closed, representing an average of two closures per year over the 27 year period.[3] The years 1967 and 1983 seem to have been banner years for Black hospital closings, with nine hospitals closed in each year. From 1983 to 1988, 16 Black hospitals closed, including several of the most historically significant Black hospitals. Forest Avenue Hospital in Dallas, Texas, closed in 1984; Flint-Goodridge Hospital of Dillard University in New Orleans closed in May 1985;[4] and Provident Hospital in Chicago closed in September 1987.[5] The John A. Andrews Hospital (Tuskegee, Alabama) also closed in 1987.[6] Provident and John A. Andrews had provided service for nearly a century, Provident since 1891 and John A. Andrews since 1892. Provident Hospital (Baltimore) merged with Lutheran Hospital

(Baltimore) in 1985. The consolidation agreement that took effect on July 1, 1986, meant the end of Provident Hospital as an autonomous Black institution.[7] The hospital had been under severe financial strain in recent years.[8] The Hospital of Englewood (Chicago) closed in 1988.[9]

Cook County Hospital (Chicago) and Kings County Hospital (Brooklyn, New York) are among the largest hospitals with a significant Black constituency. Both hospitals have operating budgets that have exceeded $100 million.[10] Jackson Park Hospital (Chicago) and Provident Hospital (Baltimore) in the early 1980s were the largest private nonteaching Black hospitals.[11] Table 5.1 shows that 26 Black hospitals were in existence in 1988. These hospitals are categorized by Wesley and Link as traditional Black private hospitals (9), transitional Black hospitals (6), and traditional Black public hospitals (11).[12] Table 5.2 lists Black hospital closings and transitions between 1961 and 1988.

Provident Hospital (Chicago) had opened a new 300-bed facility in 1983 after years of having an obsolete physical plant that had been cited for health and safety code violations.[13] Yet, this new, ultramodern facility was unable to bring about an increase in its occupancy rate or number of paying patients. By 1987, about 75 percent of the hospital's patients recieved some kind of public assistance and another 8 percent were uninsured.[14] At about that time, the hospital was forced into bankruptcy because of a $40 million debt.[15]

INTEGRATION, MEDICARE/MEDICAID POLICIES AND THE DECLINE OF THE BLACK HOSPITAL

Of the several explanations as to why Black hospitals have closed, two of the most important are (1) integration and its resultant attitudinal changes among the Black population regarding health care and (2) the advent of Medicare/Medicaid programs. Integration has served as a double-edged sword for Black hospitals. "Black hospitals were built to serve Blacks because Black patients and medical staff could not use segregated facilities run by Whites."[16] Roylance points out that in 1960 in Baltimore, Maryland, only 1,000 of the estimated

Table 5.1
Black Hospitals, 1988

NAME	LOCATION
Bethany Hospital**	Chicago
Charity Hospital of Louisiana***	New Orleans
Cook County Hospital***	Chicago
Cuyahoga County Hospital***	Cleveland
D. C. General Hospital***	District of Columbia
Detroit Receiving Hospital***	Detroit
George W. Hubbard Hospital	Nashville, TN
of Meharry Medical College*	
Harlem Hospital Center***	New York City
Howard University Hospital*	District of Columbia
Hughes-Spalding Community Hospital*	Atlanta
Jackson Park Hospital**	Chicago
Kings County Hospital Center***	Brooklyn, NY
King-Drew Medical Center***	Los Angeles
L. Richardson Memorial Hospital	Greensboro, NC
Memphis Hospitals***	Memphis
(Regional Medical Center)	
Norfolk Community Hospitals*	Norfolk, VA
North General Hospital**	New York City
Richmond Community Hospital*	Richmond, VA
Riverside General Hospital*	Houston
Roseland Community Hospital**	Chicago
Southwest Community Hospital**	Atlanta
Southwest Detroit Hospital**	Detroit
St. Bernard Hospital**	Chicago
University Hospital (CMDN)****	Newark
Westland Medical Center ***	Westland, MI
Whittaker Memorial Hospital	Newport News, VA
(Newport News General	
Hospital,* effective 1985)	

Source: Derived from Nathaniel Wesley, Jr., *1984 Black Hospitals Listing and Selected Commentary* (Washington, D.C.: Howard University, 1984), pp. 17-20; Frank D. Roylance, "Black Hospitals in Critical Conditions." *Baltimore Evening Sun*, September 23-36, 1985, four-part series; and Nathaniel R. Wesley, Jr., and Julie Benton Lynk, "Institutional Survival: Barriers to the Survival of Black and Other Health Care Facilities and Institutions Serving Predominantly Black Populations," paper presented at the Harlem Hospital Centennial National Health Conference, April 22-23, 1988, New York City.

*Traditional black private hospitals = 9; **Transitional black hospitals = 6; ***Traditional black public hospitals = 11; N = 26.

Table 5.2
Black Hospital Closings and Transitions, 1961-1988

NAME	LOCATION	YEAR FOUNDED	YEAR CLOSED
St. Agnes Hospital	Raleigh, NC	1896	1961
Pinkston Clinic Hospital	Dallas, TX	1927	1961
Parkside Hospital	Detroit, MI	1918	1963
Brewster Hospital	Jacksonville, AL	1930	1963
Provident Hospital	Ft. Lauderdale, FL	1938	1964
McRae Memorial Sanitarium	Alexander, AR	1931	1965
Holy Family Hospital	Ensley, AL	1946	1965
Mercy Hospital	Wilson, NC	1930	1965
Good Shephard Hospital	New Bern, NC	1937	1966
Good Samaritan Hospital	Charlotte, NC	1881	1966
Shaw Memorial Hospital	Oxford, NC	1953	1967
Hunter Clinic Hospital	Marlin, TX	1923	1967
St. Martin Porres Hospital	Mobile, AL	1950	1967
Jefferson Co. TB Hospital	Beaumont, TX	1924	1967
Moton Memorial Hospital	Tulsa, OK	1931	1967
Community Hospital	Wilmington, NC	1920	1967
Jubilee Hospital	Henderson, NC	1911	1967
Gaston Co. Negro Hospital	Gastonia, NC	1911	1967
People's Hospital	St. Louis, MO	19??	1967
St. Phillips Hospital	Richmond, VA	--	1968 (Merger)
St. Mary's Infirmary	St. Louis, MO	1877	1969
Dr. E.R. Noble Clinic Hospital	Rosedale, MS	1918	1970
Collins Chapel Hospital	Memphis, TN	1909	1971
Florida A&M Univ. Hospital	Tallahassee, FL	1911	1972

Table 5.2 Continued

Mercy-Douglass Hospital (1895-1948)	Philadelphia	1895	1973
Good Samaritan Waverly Hospital	Columbia, SC	1910	1974
Kate Biting Reynolds Memorial Hospital	Winston-Salem, NC	1938	1974 (Consolidation)
E.H. Crump Hospital	Memphis, TN	1897	1974 (Consolidation)
Burton Mercy Hospital	Detroit, MI	1939	1974 (Merger)
Boulevard General Hospital	Detroit, MI	1933	1974 (Merger)
Whitney M. Young, Jr. Hospital	Los Angeles, CA	--	1975
Hancock Memorial Hospital	Sparta, GA	--	1975
Red Cross Hospital	Louisville, KY	1899	1975
Yazoo Clinic Hospital	Yazoo City, MS	1940	1975
Lincoln Hospital	Durham, NC	1901	1976 (Consolidation)
Mercy General Hospital	Detroit, MI	1918	1976
Morrisania City Hospital	Bronx, NY	1929	1976
Highland Park Gen. Hospital	Highland Park, MI	1920	1976
McClendon-Banks Mem. Hospital	Charleston, SC	1959	1977
Douglass Hospital	Kansas City, MO	1898	1977
St. Joseph Hospital	Kansas City, MO	1874	1977 (Consolidation)
Forest City Hospital	Cleveland, OH	1957	1977
Tabernacle Community Hospital	Chicago, IL	1910	1977
West Adams Community Hospital	Los Angeles, CA	--	1978 (Consolidation)
Arthur C. Logan Hospital	New York, NY	1862	1978
Burrell Memorial Hospital	Roanoke, VA	1915	1979
Homer G. Phillips Hospital	St. Louis, MO	1937	1979
Sydenham Hospital	New York, NY	1927	1980 (Conversion)
Detroit Receiving Hospital	Detroit, MI	1915	1980 (Conversion)

Table 5.2 Continued

Morningside Hospital	Los Angeles, CA	1958	1980
Lockwood Hospital	Houston, TX	1957	1981
Community Hospital of Evanston	Evanston, IL	1930	1981 (Conversion)
Clement Atkinson Mem. Hospital	Coatesville, PA	1937	1981
Jackson Hospital	Terrell, TX	--	1983
Kessler Hospital	Dallas, TX	--	1983
Riverside Adventist Hospital	Nashville, TN	1927	1983
Cumberland Hospital	Brooklyn, NY	1922	1983
Good Samaritan Hospital and Nursing Home	Selma, AL	1944	1983
Flint General Hospital	Flint, MI	1932	1983
Christian Hospital	Miami, FL	1918	1983
Mound Bayou Community Hospital	Mound Bayou, MS	1942	1983
MLK Jr. Memorial Hospital	Kansas City, MO	1918	1983
Forest Avenue Hospital	Dallas, TX	1966	1984
Flint-Goodridge Hospital	New Orleans, LA	1932	1985
Provident Hospital	Baltimore, MD	1894	1986 (Merged)
Fairview Medical Center	Montgomery, AL	1951	1986
Provident Hosptial	Chicago, IL	1891	1987
John A. Andrews Hospital	Tuskegee, AL	1912	1987
Milton Community Hospital	River Rouge, MI	1938	1987
The Hospital of Englewood	Chicago, IL	--	1988

Source: Same as Table 5.1.

5,200 beds were open to Blacks.[17] Provident Hospital, Baltimore's major Black hospital in 1960, was a 137-bed facility that had been described as "grossly inadequate" to serve the needs of the city's Black population. Although some beds were available to Blacks at other hospitals in the city of Baltimore, according to Roylance, "Most private hospitals either excluded Blacks or relegated them to a fixed number of beds in segregated wards."[18]

Integration, and the advent of the Medicare/Medicaid programs have made Black hospitals and Black patients both victims and beneficiaries. Andre Lee has noted that, "while on the one hand these programs have enabled black patients the access to White institutions, they simultaneously diminished the use of these [black] hospitals by black physicians and their patients both public assistance and self pay patients."[19] It is ironic, then, that while Medicare/Medicaid programs provided health coverage to a large number of uninsured persons, these same programs have served as a basis for denial of hospital services by a large number of hospitals, especially for-profit ones.[20] Allegedly, limited government reimbursement schedules under these programs did not allow hospitals to keep charges above costs. As a result, for-profit/proprietary hospitals have attempted to limit the number of Medicare/Medicaid patients they serve because treating them has been an economic disincentive.[21] Public hospitals then have carried the burden of providing care to Medicare/Medicaid recipients as well as to those patients who are uninsured.

In California in 1979 Medicare and Medical (Medicaid) reimbursed hospitals at 4 percent and 18 percent less than their costs, respectively. In county hospitals the patient-care revenues received were 27 percent less than the costs.[22] Public hospitals are thus put at a severe financial disadvantage in serving Medicare/Medicaid recipients because of reimbursement schedules that are set below the cost of actually providing the service and because care is not readily accessible to the poor from private, for-profit hospitals. In many cities and counties the public hospital is the only department that operates in the red. Stated another way, local governments find it difficult to match their principal source of revenue, the property tax, against their most rapidly increasing expenditure, hospital costs.

Local governments have become unwilling, because of fiscal pressures to continue to subsidize the costs of their hospitals. Public hospitals with a large Black consistency, such as Homer G. Phillips Hospital in St. Louis and Philadelphia General Hospital, have been closed as a result of government action. Charity Hospital in New Orleans, D.C. General Hospital in Washington, D\C., and Boston City Hospital, all public hospitals, were so inadequately funded at one time that they lost their accreditation by the Joint Commission on Accreditation of Hospitals.[23] Each of these hospitals served a large Black population. Further, California's public hospital system shrunk from 65 hospitals operated by 49 counties (out of a total of 58 counties) in 1964, to 37 hospitals in 29 counties in 1982 and to 31 hospitals in 1985.[24] The thirty-four closed hospitals provided care to a large black and other minority population. Cook County hospital in Chicago, which provides services to a largely Black and poor clientele has been on the brink of closure several times. Other public hospitals have followed a similar course. Hospitals that receive a large share of their revenues from state and local appropriations are particularly vulnerable to the vagaries of local economies and politics.[25]

Further, many of the few remaining Black hospitals are in financial stress. Patients of Black hospitals are typically minorities and poor individuals who either cannot pay for care or are Medicare/Medicaid recipients. Provident Hospital (Baltimore) in 1984, at the time struggling to remain financially solvent, had the third highest percentage of charity cases and bad debts of its total budget of all 52 hospitals in Maryland.[26] Howard University Hospital in Washington, D.C., in 1984 provided $25 million in charity care, a quarter of the charity care provided in the metropolitan D.C. area.[27]

A growing body of research now argues that the higher the amount of a hospital's charity care and/or Medicaid patients the more likely it is to have financial stress. For example, Feder, Hadley, and Mullner, after analyzing data from 1,125 respondent hospitals, concluded that "the probability of financial stress was two times larger for hospitals heavily involved in serving the poor than for other hospitals."[28] In California a report by the California Hospital Association noted that Medi-Cal (California's Medicaid program) may be dangerous to a hospital's fiscal health. The report specifically pointed out that "the more income a hospital gets from Medi-Cal, the more its financial health seems to deteriorate."[29] Friedman observed that a Medicaid percentage of 50 percent or more means financial trouble for a Black hospital. This is especially the case for the small Black hospital. As Friedman notes, "The size of the facility is important; if the hospital is larger, the survival time is longer, because it has more resources."[30]

Despite these observations, the fiscal stress of Provident Hospital (Chicago) as a result of charity care dates as far back as the late 1940s. In July 1949 the outpatient department at Provident was closed because of inadequate financial resources.[31] For approximately 13,000 visits annually for emergency care, only about 25 percent of patients paid anything and less than 10 percent paid full cost. About 93 percent of the clinic visits were furnished to public and private agency patients whose payments were only about 33 percent of cost. Hospital funds were used to meet the remaining 67 percent. For inpatient care, public and private agency patients and free and part pay patients represented about 26 percent.[32]

ATTITUDES OF THE BLACK COMMUNITY

The other explanation for the decline of the Black hospital has more to do with the attitudes of the Black community to include both Black physicians and Black patients. Black physicians, who once were denied practice and admitting privileges, suddenly had access to White facilities. As many Black hospitals are inadequately equipped, many Black physicians and their patients willingly use White hospitals because of access to better equipment, library resources, and physical structures, not to mention their sense of a right to practice in modern, well-appointed facilities.[33] Once they have access to White facilities, Black physicians admit Black patients who are able to pay or who are insured through commercial insurance programs. Black and White physicians, because of the policies of for-profit/proprietary hospitals, admit their indigent patients to Black, charity, or public hospitals. Further, the Black middle class has sought out the White hospital; the patients left behind are the poor, the elderly, the penniless, and Medicare/Medicaid recipients. Moreover, some Blacks hold the attitude "that something is better because it's White."[34] Thus, "being 'black' can stigmatize a hospital among many Blacks, just as it does among many Whites."[35]

CONCLUDING OBSERVATIONS AND RECOMMENDATIONS

This book has discussed public policy and the history, development, and decline of the Black hospital in the United States. Discriminatory segregation policies and practices promoted the development and growth of the Black hospital from the slavery period through the mid 1960s. In the mid-1960s court action and federal integration policy along with the advent of Medicare/Medicaid programs opened the once-closed doors of White hospitals to Black doctors and Black patients. These activities seem to be largely responsible for the decline of the Black hospital in the 1980s and 1990s. Yet, one may ask, "So what?" Are services and care not available to Blacks from other hospitals? Why should the decline of the Black hospital be an important issue in the Black community?

Public hospitals, which constitute about one-third of the community hospitals in the United States and are the principal health resource available to the black community, have been declining in number.[36] Yet local governments are reducing their capacity to support public hospitals because in many instances public hospitals are becoming too expensive to fund and operate.[37] At the same time, a large number of public hospitals are being sold or leased to private, for-profit or proprietary chains, and hospital care is increasingly being provided by these chains. As was noted earlier, private, for-private hospitals limit service to or consider it fiscally imprudent to serve the poor and Medicare/Medicaid recipients. Further, private, for-profit hospitals are rapidly growing in number. In 1984 the four largest for-profit chains (Hospital Corporation of America, American Medical International Inc., Humana Inc., and National Medical Enterprises Inc.) owned 709 hospitals with 105,000 beds; managed another 250 hospitals with nearly 32,000 beds; and owned 11 primary-provider organizations, 58 psychiatric hospitals, and 20 health maintenance organizations.[38] Proprietary institutions in 1984 owned some 20 percent of the market, about double the market share in 1979.[39] It is estimated that by the early 1990s 30 percent of all acute-care hospitals will be proprietary.[40]

Further, Blacks, like every other minority group, need institutions they can call their own; a hospital is perhaps one of the most serviceable institutions a minority group can have. The symbolic functions of a hospital for the Black community are important. To name a few, a Black hospital constitutes a resource for leadership, a focal point for community interests, devotion, and need; and at least one assurance of having arrived in the American political/economic system.

How are the few remaining Black hospitals to survive? What survival strategies are necessary? According to Roylance, "developing specialty areas" is the key to Black hospital survival.[41] This is necessary to attract patients of all colors. Specialties may include such areas as geriatric medicine (Hubbard Hospital of Meharry Medical School), an outpatient facility (Flint General Hospital), and a community-based alcoholism and drug addiction treatment facility (Sydenham Hospital and Kirkwood General Hospital). Another alternative is for specialty Black hospitals to become the counterpart of major well-known specialty White hospitals-remain nearly separate but become truly equal-and develop national or regional appeal to Black doctors and prospective Black patients because of their specialty services. This is to say that a specialty Black hospital has to become the first choice of a very large number of Blacks needing medical service.

Further, if Black hospitals can develop separate specialty areas, they may be able to attract different segments of the Black community and thus reduce competition among themselves for patients from the Black community at-large. Another strategy may involve mergers or alliances with other institutions. This may be most applicable in communities where more than one small Black hospital exists. In 1974 Boulevard General and Burton Mercy Hospitals merged to form Southwest Detroit Hospital.[42]   Cook County Hospital formed an alliance to buy a small number of beds and to refer patients with certain diagnoses to Provident Hospital (Chicago).[43]   Ultimately, Black hospitals must take these and other actions if they are to survive into the twenty-first century.

Finally, the federal government can deal with the problem of declining Black hospitals by creating a reimbursement system under a national health system in which all hospitals split the costs of uncompensated care through a government centered hospital system providing universal coverage.[44] For public hospitals and Black hospitals, this would eliminate, or at least reduce the pressure caused by competition for paying patients their most crucial need.

NOTES

1. Nathaniel Wesley, Jr., *1984 Black Hospitals Listing and Selected Commentary* (Washington, DC: Howard University, 1984).

2. Ibid. pp. 3-20.

3. Ibid. pp. 4-21.

4. F. D. Roylance, "Provident Survives While Others Shut Down." *Baltimore Evening Sun* (September 23, 1985): A1, A4.

5. See Nathaniel R. Wesley Jr. and Julit Benton Link, "Institutional Survival: Barriers to the Survival of Black and Other Health Care Facilities and Institutions Serving Predominantly Black Populations." Paper presented at the Harlem Hospital Centennial National Health Conference, April 22-23, 1988, New York, NY; and John Kass, "Provident Staff Told Ax in Mail." *Chicago Tribune* (December 16, 1987): 1,9.

6. "Hospital to Keep Operating." *Montgomery Advertiser* (September 29, 1987): 1,7.

7. Editor, "Court Approves Merger of Provident Hospital and Lutheran Hospital in Baltimore." *The NRW Report* (August 1986): 1.

8. Joseph M. Miller, "Demise of Provident Hospital." *Journal of the National Medical Association* 78 (1986): 919-920.

9. Wesley and Link, "Institutional Survival," p. 31.

10. Wesley, *1984 Black Hospitals Listing and Selected Commentary*, pp. 22-23.

11. Ibid. p. 32.

12. Wesley and Link, "Institutional Survival," p. 16.

13. "The New Provident Hospital Medical Center." *Journal of the National Medical Association* 75 (1983): 727.

14. Deborah Pinkey, "Future Looks Bleak for Black Hospitals."
American Medical News 10 (April 1987): 50.
15. "Provident Hospital Shutting Down." *Chicago Tribune*
(September 15, 1987): 2.
16. R. C. Lokeman, "Many Black Hospitals Face Critical Times."
Kansas City Star (December 7, 1983).
17. Roylance, "Provident Survives While Others Shut Down," A1,
A4.
18. Ibid.
19. Andre L. Lee, "Black Community Hospitals: A Quest for
Survival." *Urban Health* (March 1984): 46-47.
20. E. R. Brown, "Public Hospitals on the Brink: Their Problems
and Their Options." *Journal of Health Politics, Policy and Law*
(Winter 1983):   927-944; and Geraldine Dallek, "The Continuing
Plight of Hospitals." *Clearinghouse Review* (June 1982): 97-101.
21. Mitchell F. Rice, "The Urban Public Hospital: Its Importance
to the Black Community." *Urban League Review* 9 (Winter 1985/86):
64-70; and National Health Law Program, "For Profit Hospitals and
the Poor." *Clearinghouse Review* (December 1982): 860-86.
22. Brown, "Public Hospitals on Brink," 933-935; and Geraldine
Dallek, "Health Care for America's Poor: Separate and Unequal."
Clearinghouse Review 20 (Summer of 1986): 361-371.
23. J. G. Haughton, "Municipal Hospitals: Their Relevance to the
Black Community." *Urban League Review* 4 (Summer 199): 25-28.
24.   Brown, "Public Hospitals on the Brink," 933-935 and
Geraldine Dallek, "Health Care for America's Poor: Separate and
Unequal," pp. 361-371.
25. Brown, "Public Hospitals on the Brink," pp. 932-937.
26. F. D. Roylance, "Provident Seeking Allegiance of Blacks."
Baltimore Evening Sun (September 24, 1985): A1,A4.
27. Ibid.
28. J. Feder Hadley and R. Mullner, "Poor People and Poor
Hospitals: Implications for Public Policy." *Journal of Health
Politics*, Policy and Law (Summer 1984): 237-250.
29. "Warning: Medi-Cal May Be Dangerous to Your Health."
CHA Insight (September 3, 1980): 2-5.

30. Emily Friedman, "Private Black Hospitals: A Long Tradition Facing Change." *Hospitals* 52 (July 1, 1978): 63-68.

31. Clyde L. Reynolds, "The Fiscal Results of Segregation." *The Modern Hospital* 76 (6) (June 1951): 64.

32. Ibid.

33. Lee, "Black Community Hospitals," p. 47.

34. Quote of Nathaniel Wesley, Jr., cited in Friedman, "Private Black Hospitals," p. 64.

35. Roylance, "Provident Seeking Allegiance of Blacks," A1, A4. See also LaRah D. Payne, "Survival of Black Hospitals in the U.S. Health Care System: A Case Study." In Lennox S. Yearwood (ed.), *Black Organizations: Issues in Survival Techniques* (Lanham, MD: University Press of America, 1980).

36. Brown, "Public Hospitals on the Brink," pp. 929-936.

37. Rice, "The Urban Public Hospital," pp. 67-69; and D. H. Hitt and R. B. Sullivan, "Multi-Institutional Arrangements: Ownership Issues Confront Community Hospitals," *Hospitals* (July 16, 1985): 69-84.

38. S. Martin and J. Gooderis, "Policy and Structural Change in Health Care Industry." *Antitrust Bulletin* (Winter 1985): 949-974.

39. "Medicine." *Time* (December 10, 1984): 84.

40. National Health Law Program, "For Profit Hospitals and the Poor," pp. 862-864.

41. F. D. Roylance, "Developing Specialty Areas Key to Survival." *Baltimore Evening Sun* (September 26, 1985): A1, A4.

42. Ibid.

43. Ibid.

44. H. Morone and G. Dunham, "Slouching Toward a National Health Insurance: The New Health Care Politics." *Yale Journal of Regulation* 2 (1985): 263-285.

Appendix — Black Hospitals in the United States

STATE AND NAME OF HOSPITAL

ALABAMA	CITIES
Holy Family Hospital	Endlsey
Bienville Infirmary	Mobile
Burwell's Infirmary	Selma
Cottage Home Infirmary	Decatur
Oakwood Jr. College Sanitarium	Huntsville
Hale's Infirmary	Montgomery
Fraternity Hospital	Montgomery
Northcross Sanitarium	Montgomery
Colored Infirmary	Eufaula
John A. Andrew Memorial Hospital	Talledega
Fairview Medical Center*	Tuskegee
Virginia McCormick Hospital	Normal
George Cleveland Hall Hospital	Birmingham
Children's Home Hospital	Birmingham
Negro Baptist Hospital	Selma
Government Hospital for Disabled Soldiers (Veterans' Hosp.)	Tuskegee
St. Martin Porres Hospital	Mobile
John F. Taylor Hospital	Mobile
Harris Sanitorium	Mobile
Northside Hospital	Birmingham
Tuggle Institute Hospital	Birmingham
Good Samaritan Hospital	Selma
Goodnow Hospital	Talladega
Searcy Hospital	Mt. Vernon

| Goodnow Hospital | Talladega |
| Searcy Hospital | Mt. Vernon |

ARIZONA

| Booker T. Washington Hospital | Phoenix |

ARKANSAS

Lena Jordan Hospital	Little Rock
Royal Circle of Friends Hospital	Hot Springs
Phythian Sanitarium	Hot Springs
Bush Memorial Hospital	Little Rock
Fraternal Hospital	Little Rock
Mosaic State Hospital	Little Rock
Lucy Memorial Hospital	Pine Bluff
United Friends Hospital	Little Rock
Colored Sanitarium	Little Rock
Circle of United Links State Hospital	Pine Bluff
Woodmen of Union Hospital	Hot Springs
McRae Memorial Sanitarium	Alexander
Negro Infirmary and Training School	Little Rock

CALIFORNIA

Morningside Hospital	L.A.
Dunbar Hospital	L.A.
Whitney M. Young, Jr. Hospital	L.A.
West Adams Community Hospital	L.A.
MLK Jr. General Hospital*	L.A.

COLORADO

| National Sanitarium for Colored | Co. Springs |
| National Lincoln Sanitarium for Negroes | Co. Springs |

DISTRICT OF COLUMBIA
Howard University Hospital*
Burwell Private Hospital
Carson's Private Hospital

Adam's Private Hospital
Curtis Private Sanitarium
Dowling's Private Sanitarium
D.C. General Hospital*
Francis Hospital

DELAWARE
Edgewood Sanitarium   Marshalltown

FLORIDA
Mercy Hospital   Ocala
Brewster Hospital   Jacksonville
Blue Circle Hospital   Palatka
Christian Hospital   Miami
City Hospital for Colored   Lakeland
Clara Fyre Hospital   Tampa
McCleod Hospital   Daytona
Negro Hospital   Ft. Lauderdale
Pine Ridge Hospital   W. Palm Beach
Mary Lawson Sanitarium   Palatka
Venzuella E. Small Hospital   Tampa
Provident Hospital   Tallahassee
Halifax Hospital   Daytona Beach
Tampa Negro Hospital   Tampa

GEORGIA
Burrus's Sanitarium   Augusta
Charity Hospital   Savannah
Dr. George W. Evans Sanitarium   Lithonia
East Side Sanitarium   Savannah
Georgia Infirmary ***   Savannah
Lamar Hospital   Augusta
McVicar Hospital   Atlanta
Fair Haven Hospital   Atlanta
William A. Harris Memorial Hospital   Atlanta
Americus Colored Hospital   Americus

Brookhaven Sanitarium	Raine
Johnson Memorial Hospital	Bainbridge
Bruce Hospital	Augusta
Southwest Community Hospital*	Atlanta
Dunbar Hospital	Atlanta
Jackson Hospital**	Augusta
Dwelle's Sanitarium	Atlanta
East Side Sanitarium	Savannah
Frederick and Strickland Hospital	Valdosta
Lundy Colored Hospital	Macon
Mercy Hospital	Atlanta
St. Luke Hospital	Macon
Van Buren Sanitarium	Statesboro
Statesboro Hospital	Statesboro
W. A. Harris Memorial Hospital	Atlanta
Samaritan Hospital	Rome
Grady Hospital	Atlanta
Hancock Memorial Hospital	Sparta
Hughes-Spalding Pavilion of Grady Hospital	Atlanta
Gillespie Hospital	Cordele
Evanston Sanitarium	Evanston
Provident Hospital	Chicago
The Wilson Hospital	Chicago
Bethany Hospital*	Chicago
Home Sanitarium	Jacksonville
Cook County Hospital*	Chicago
Ft. Dearborn Hospital	Chicago
Jackson Park Hospital*	Chicago
Daily Hospital	Chicago
Hinsdale Sanitarium	Hinsdale
Community Hospital	Evanston
Home Sanitarium	Chicago
Roseland Community Hospital	Chicago
John T. Wilson Hospital	Chicago
Willis Physio-Therapeutic Sanitarium	Chicago
Tabernacle Community Hospital	Chicago

St. Bernard Hospital*   Chicago
Kinniebrew's Infirmary   Jacksonville

INDIANA

Charity Hospital   Indianapolis
Colored Hospital   Evansville
Provident Hospital   Indianapolis
Lincoln Hospital   Indianapolis
Community Hospital   Indianapolis
McMitchell Sanitarium   Gary
Patient Hospital   Gary
St. John Hospital   Gary
Southern Sanitarium   Martinville
Dr. Joseph H. Ward Sanitarium   Indianapolis
Hoover's Sanitarium   Terre Haute

KANSAS

Topeka Industrial Institute Hospital   Topeka
Douglas Hospital   Kansas City
Mitchell Hospital   Leavensworth
Kansas Vocational School Hospital   Topeka
Florence Crittenton Home   Topeka
Nellie Johns Memorial Hospital   Topeka

KENTUCKY

King's Daughters Hospital   Louisville
Citizen's National Hospital   Louisville
Red Cross Sanitarium Hospital   Covington
Anderson Sanitarium   Somerset
Booker T. Washington Hospital   Middlesboro
Colored Annex of Mercy Hospital   Paris
Moore Clinic   Hopkinsville
Red Cross Hospital   Louisville

LOUISIANA

Charity Hospital*   New Orleans

Dr. F. T. Jones Sanitarium	Shreveport
Provident Sanitarium	New Orleans
Flint Goodridge Hospital	New Orleans
Robinson Infirmary	New Orleans
Southern University Hospital	Scotlandville
Mercy Sanitarium	Shreveport

MARYLAND

Provident Hospital	Baltimore
Tuberculosis Hospital for Colored	Baltimore
Victory Hospital	Baltimore
Crownsville State Hospital	Waterbury
Good Shepherd General Hospital	Baltimore

MASSACHUSETTS

Garland Hospital	Boston
Plymouth Hospital	Boston

MICHIGAN

Milton Community Hospital*	River Range
Detroit Receiving Hospital*	Detroit
Dunbar Memorial Hospital	Detroit
Edyth K. Thomas Memorial Hospital	Detroit
Kirkwood General Hospital	Detroit
Flint General Hospital	Flint
Fairview Sanitarium	Detroit
Wayne Diagnostic Hospital	Detroit
Good Samaritan Hospital	Detroit
Mercy Hospital	Detroit
St. Aubin's Hospital	Detroit
Parkside Hospital	Detroit
Trinity Hospital	Detroit
Highland Park Hospital	Highland Park
Bethesda Hospital	Detroit

MISSISSIPPI

Dumas Infirmary	Natchez
Afro American Sons and	
Daughters Hospital	Yazoo City
Colored Hospital	Lexington
Dr. Miller's Hospital	Yazoo City
King's Daughter Hospital	Greenville
Mound Bayou Community Hospital	Mound Bayou
Taborian Hospital	Mound Bayou
Plantation Hospital	Scott
Rosedale Colored Hospital	Rosedale
Yazoo Clinic Hospital	Yazoo City
Greenwood Colored Hospital	Greenwood

MISSOURI

Colored Maternity Home and Infirmary	St. Louis
Provident Hospital	St. Louis
MLK Jr. Memorial Hospital*	Kansas City
Wheatley Provident Hospital	Kansas City
City Hospital No. 2	Sedalia
City Public Hospital for Colored	St. Louis
St. Joseph Hospital	Kansas City
Kansas City Colored Hospital	Kansas City
People's Hospital	St. Louis
Homer G. Phillips	St. Louis
St. Mary's Infirmary	St. Louis
Perry Sanitarium	Kansas City

NEW JERSEY

Booker T. Washington Hospital	Newark
Martland Hospital*	Newark
Wright Sanitarium and	
Maternity Hospital	Newark
Kenney Memorial Hospital	Newark
Community Hospital	Newark

NEW YORK

Cumberland Hospital	Brooklyn
Arthur C. Logan Hospital	New York City
Lincoln Hospital	New York City
Harlem Hospital Center*	New York City
Edgecomb Sanitarium	New York City
International Hospital	New York City
Morrisiana Hospital	Bronx
Kings County Hospital*	Brooklyn
Colored Orphan Asylum	New York City
Dr. Wiley M. Wilson Private Hospital	New York City
Sydenham Hospital	New York City
Colored Homes and Hospital	New York City

NEW MEXICO

Hawkins Sanitarium	Silver City

NORTH CAROLINA

Colored Hospital and Sanitarium	Ashville
Good Samaritan Hospital	Charlotte
Lincoln Hospital	Durham
Quality Hill Sanitarium	Monroe
Slater Hospital	Winston-Salem
St. Agnes Hospital	Raleigh
Leonard Hospital	Shaw
Mercy Hospital	Wilson
McCauley Private Hospital	Raleigh
Good Shepherd Hospital	New Bern
Shaw Memorial Hospital	Oxford
Wilson Hospital	Wilson
Katie Biting Reynolds Memorial Hospital*	Winston-Salem
Blue Ridge Hospital	Ashville
Community Hospital	Durham
County Hospital for Colored	Durham
State Hospital	Goldsboro
Gaston County Negro Hospital	Gastonia

Johnston County Hospital	Southfield
Leary-Perry Hospital	Fayetteville
N.B. Duke Memorial Orthopedic Hospital	Gastonia
Negro Community Hospital	Wilmington
Susie Clayton Cheatham Memorial Hosp.	Oxford
Rivera Clinic	Mt. Olive
Jubilee Hospital	Henderson
L. Richardson Memorial Hospital*	Greensboro
Pinehurst Infirmary	Pinehurst
Trinity Hospital	Greensboro

OHIO

Alpha Hospital	Columbus
Colley's Private Hospital	Cincinnati
Cuyahoga County Hospital*	Cleveland
Dr. H.R. Hawkins Sanitarium	Xenia
Mercy Hospital	Cincinnati
Tawawa Hospital	Wilberforce
Forest City Hospital	Cleveland
Colored Hospital	Cincinnati

OKLAHOMA

City Hospital	Baley
Dr. Conrad's Sanitarium	Guthrie
Great Western Hospital	Oklahoma City
Hubbard Memorial Clinic	Tulsa
Maurice Willows Hospital	Tulsa
Muckleberry Clinical Hospital	Muskogee
Park Sanitarium	Guthrie
Wilson Sanitarium	Tulsa
Bryant Clinic	Tulsa
City Hospital	Baley
City Hospital for Colored	Muskogee
Morrison Hospital	Muskogee
Frissel Memorial Hospital	Tulsa
Municipal Hospital #2	Tulsa

Muskogee Provident Hospital	Muskogee
Okmulgee City Colored Hospital	Okmulgee
Edwards Memorial Hospital	Oklahoma City

PENNSYLVANIA

Institution House of Good Shepherd	Philadelphia
Dr. W. C. Atkinson's Private Hospital	Coatsville
Frederick Douglass Memorial Hospital	Philadelphia
Mercy Hospital	Philadelphia
Jackson's Sanitarium	Philadelphia
Booker T. Washington Hospital	Pittsburgh
Clement Atkinson Memorial Hospital	Coatesville

SOUTH CAROLINA

Benedict College Hospital	Columbia
Booker T. Washington Hospital	Denmark
Brewer Normal School Hospital	Greenwood
Colored Hospital	Georgetown
Colored Hospital	Charleston
County Negro Hospital	Spartanburg
Lee Hospital	Summerville
Palmetto Tuberculosis Hospital	Columbia
Florence Williams Hospital	Georgetown
Provident Hospital	Spartanburg
St. Luke's Hospital	Greenville
Taylor Lane Hospital	Columbia
Mrs. Dr. Rhodes Private Hospital	Columbia
Good Samaritan Hospital	Columbia
Union Community Hospital	Union
Waverly Hospital	Columbia
Working Benevolent Hospital	Greenville
St. Luke's Hospital	Columbia
People's Infirmary	Columbia
McClendon-Banks Memorial Hospital	Charleston
Hospital and Training School for Nurses	Charleston

TENNESSEE

Harriston Infirmary	Nashville
Hadley's Private Infirmary for Women	Nashville
Brookhaven Hospital	Jackson
Collins Chapel Connectional Hospital	Memphis
Colored Hospital	Conway
Cottage Hospital	Nashville
Eliza B. Wallace Memorial Hospital	Knoxville
George W. Hubbard Hospital*	Nashville
Jane Terrell Baptist Hospital	Memphis
Lincoln County Colored Hospital	Fayetteville
Lynkrest Sanitarium	Bartlett
Maury County Negro Hospital	Columbia
McMillan Infirmary	Nashville
Mercy Hospital	Bristol
Boyds Infirmary	Nashville
Millie E. Hale Hospital	Nashville
Memphis Regional Medical Center*	Memphis
Old Folks Home and Hospital	Memphis
Friendly Clinic	Memphis
Riverside Sanitarium and Hospital	Nashville
St. Anthony's Hospital for Colored	Memphis
The Home Infirmary	Clarksville
Walden Hospital	Chattanooga
Erlanger Hospital	Chattanooga
Negro Baptist Hospital	Memphis
Rock City Sanitarium	Nashville
E. H. Crump Hospital	Memphis
Dr. J. T. Wilson's Infirmary	Nashville
Booker T. Washington Hospital	Fayetteville

TEXAS

Booker T. Washington Hospital	Ft. Worth
Dr. Sheppard's Hospital	Marshall
Jackson Hospital	Terrell
Houston Negro Hospital	Houston
St. Elizabeth Hospital	Houston

McMillan Sanitarium	Dallas
Moore Sanitarium	Galveston
Jefferson County TB Hospital	Beaumont
Prairie View College Hospital	Prairie View
Forest Avenue Hospital	Dallas
Hubbard Sanitarium	Galveston
Kessler Hospital	Dallas
Standard Sanitarium	Marlin
People's Sanitarium	Houston
Tent Colony for Colored People	San Antonio
Lockwood Hospital	Houston
Physicians and Surgeons Infirmary	San Antonio
Union Hospital	Houston
Riverside General Hospital*	Houston
Watts Sanitarium for Colored People	Houston
Pinkston Clinic Hospital	Dallas
Hunter Clinic Hospital	Marlin
Negro Tuberculosis Hospital	Ft. Worth
Feagin's Hospital	Houston
Ethel Ransom Memorial Hospital	Ft. Worth
Colored Hospital	Dallas

VIRGINIA

Burrell-Memorial Hospital	Roanoke
Central State Hospital	Petersburg
Dixie Hospital	Hampton
Epps Memorial Hospital	Petersburg
Richmond Hospital*	Richmond
Tidewater Hospital	Norfolk
St. Mary's Hospital	Martinville
Loulie Taylor Letcher Memorial Hospital	Lawrenceville
Norfolk Community Hospital*	Norfolk
Piedmont Sanitarium	Burkesville
St. Phillip Hospital	Richmond
Sarah G. Jones Memorial Hospital	Richmond
Whittaker Memorial Hospital*	Richmond
Christianburg Industrial Institute Hospital	Christianburg

Providence Hospital   Danville

WEST VIRGINIA

North Mountain Sanitarium	North Mountain
Mercer Hospital	Bluefield
Harrison Hospital	Kimball
Barnett Hospital	Huntington
Henrietta Dismukes Hospital	Kimball
Lomax Sanitarium	Bluefield
State Colored Tuberculosis Sanitarium	Denmar
Providence Hospital	Bluefield

---

*Denotes Black hospitals and public hospitals with a large Black constituency still in operation and practice.

**Believed to be the first hospital in the United States to care for Black patients.

***Believed to be the first hospital in the United States founded for Blacks.

Sources: Compiled from Monroe Work (ed.). The Negro Yearbook: 1912, 1917, 1922, 1931, 1937, (Tuskegee, AL: Tuskegee Institute, 1912, 1917, 1922, 1931, 1937); Guzman, J. P. Negro Yearbook: 1941-1946 (Tuskegee, AL: Tuskegee Institute, 1947). Nathaniel Wesley, Jr., 1984 Black Hospitals Listing and Selected Commentary (Washington, D C: Howard University, 1984), pp. 17-20; Bubois, Frank D. Roylance, "Black Hospitals in Critical Conditions." Baltimore Evening Sun (September 23-26, 1985); Florence Murray, "Hospital," The Negro Handbook (New York: Wendell Malliet and Co., 1942); and other various sources.

Note: A few hospitals listed were white hospitals with designated beds and segregated areas for Blacks (i.e., State Hospital, NC; Searcy Hospital, AL; Central State Hospital, VA; St. Phillip Hospital, VA; Hughes-Spalding Pavilion of Grady Hospital, Atlanta, GA.

Selected Bibliography

"Access to a Hospital for Every Race Doctor." *Journal of the National Medical Association* 38 (January 1946): 35-36.

"Accommodations for Negroes." *Modern Hospital* 59 (July 1942): 40.

Adams, Numa P. G. "An Interpretation of the Significance of the Homer G. Phillips Hospital." *Journal of the National Medical Association* 26 (January/March 1934): 13-17.

Adams, Numa P. G. "Sources of Supply of Negro Health Personnel. Section A: Physicians." *Journal of Negro Education* 6 (1937): 468-76.

"Additions to Hospitals." *Journal of the National Medical Association* 22 (1930): 240.

"An Advance for Negro Health." *Modern Hospital* 62 (February 1944): 42.

Alexander, W. G. "Our Hospital Number." *Journal of the National Medical Association* 22 (July/September 1930): 140-41.

"The All-Negro Hospital." Editorial. *Southern Hospitals* 19 (September 1951): 90.

Babow, I. "Minority Group Integration in Hospitals: A Sample Survey." *Hospitals* 35 (February 1964): 47-48.

Barkholz, David. "New Urgency To Form Black Hospital System." *Modern Healthcare* (February 1985): 28.

Barrett, W.H.A. "The Missouri Hospital Situation." *Journal of the National Medical Association* 22 (July/September 1930): 148.

"Baton Rouge Hospitals Integrate." *Journal of the National Medical Association* 56 (September 1964): 447.

Bethea, Dennis A. "Some Significant Negro Movements to Lower Their Mortality." *Journal of the National Medical Association* 22 (1930): 85-88.

Bluestone, E. M. "Segregation Is an Anachronism." *Modern Hospital* 76 (June 1951): 55.

Boas, Ernst P. "The Cost of Medical Care as a Factor in the Availability of Health Facilities for Negroes." *Journal of Negro Education* 18 (19498): 333-39.

Bousfield, M. O. "Hospitals and Health Centers." *Journal of the National Medical Association* 39 (1947): 3-7.

Bradley, Eugene H. "Health, Hospitals and the Negro." *Modern Hospital* 65 (August 1945): 43-44.

Bright, M. H. "The Houston Negro Hospital." *Journal of the National Medical Association* 22 (July/September 1930): 148.

Brown, L. G. "The Hospital Problem of Negro Physicians." *Journal of the National Medical Association* 34 (March 1942): 83-85.

Browne, H. A. "A Brief History of McRae Memorial Sanatorium." *Journal of the National Medical Association* 54 (July 1962): 517-19.

Calvet, Innis. "Integration in Hospitals." *Interracial Review* 35 (July 1962): 25-35.

Cannon, J. Alfred. "The Last Economic Alternative for the Black Community." *Journal of the National Medical Association* 63 (1972): 458-59.

Carnegie, Amos H. "But Integration Is Empty Talk." *Modern Hospital* 76 (June 1951): 55-56, 142.

Carnegie, Amos H. "Not Negro Hospitals-But Hospitals." *Modern Hospital* 79 (August 1952): 76.

Carnegie, Amos H. "Washington Proposal for Self-Help." *Modern Hospital* 79 (August 1952): 76-77.

Carney, E. R. "The Care of the Negro's Health Problem Is One of Today's Problems." *Hospital Management* 48 (September 1939): 22, 65.

Carney, E R. "Directory of Negro Hospitals in the United States," 1938.

Carney, E. R. "Hospital Care for Negroes." *National Negro Health News* 10 (January-March 1942): 44-46.

Carter, Elmer A. "Race Prejudice in Municipal Hospitals." Editorial. *Opportunity* 19 (1941): 227.

"Catholic Hospital Association Passes Anti-Discrimination Resolution." *Journal of the National Medical Association* 47 (September 1963): 440.

"Changes in Negro Hospitals." *Trained Nurse and Hospital Review* 87 (1931): 196-99, 213.

"Charitable Segregation." *The Fraternal Review* 10 (January 1931).

"Chicago Activity against Hospital Discrimination Continues." *Journal of the National Medical Association* 47 (July 1955): 264-67.

"Civil Rights and Wrongs." Editorial. *Modern Hospital* 101 (October 1964): 93-94.

Cobb, William Montague. "Burrell Memorial Hospital, Roanoke, Virginia." *Journal of the National Medical Association* 55 (May 1963): 256-57.

Cobb, William Montague. "The Negro Physician and Hospital Staffs." *Hospital Management* 89 (March 1960): 22-24.

Cobb, William Montague. "Hospital Integration in the United States: A Progress Report." *Journal of the National Medical Association* 55 (July 1963): 333-37.

Cobb, William Montague. "Saint Agnes Hospital, Raleigh, North Carolina, 1896-1961." *Journal of the National Medical Association* (September 1961): 439-46.

Cobb, William Montague. "A Short History of Freedmen's Hospital." *Journal of the National Medical Association* 54 (May 1962: 271-87.

Cobb, William Montague (ed). "Integration in Medicine: A National Need." *Journal of the National Medical Association* 49 (January 1957): 1-71.

Cobb, William Montague. "The Future of Negro Medical Organizations." *Journal of the National Medical Association* 43 (1951): 323-28.

Cobb, William Montague. *Medical Care and the Plight of the Negro.* New York: National Association for the Advancement of Colored People, 1947. Excerpted in *Crisis* 54 (1947): 201-11.

Cobb, William Montague. "Medical Care for Minority Groups." *Annals of the American Academy of Political and Social Science* 273 (1951): 169-75.

Cobb, William Montague. "Old Clothes to Sam: The Negro Hospital Dilemma." *Bulletin of the Medico-Chirurgical Society of the District of Columbia* 4 (February 1947).

Cobb, William Montague. *Progress and Portents for the Negro in Medicine.* New York: National Association for the Advancement of Colored People, 1948. Excerpted in *Crisis* 55 (April 1948): 107-22, 125-26.

Cobb, William Montague. "Report of the Council of Medical Association, NMA." *Journal of the National Medical Association* 46 (1954): 440-41.

Cobb, William Montague. "Separate But Equal Facilities." *Bulletin of the Medico-Chirurgical Society of the District of Columbia* 4 (March 1947).

Cobb, William Montague. "Special Problems in the Provision of Medical Services for Negroes." *Journal of Negro Education* 18 (1949): 340-45.

Cobb, William Montague. "National Health Program of the National Association for the Advancement of Colored People." *Journal of the National Medical Association* 45 (1953): 333-39.

"Comments on Hospital Report." *Journal of the National Medical Association* 23 (1931): 190.

Commission on Hospital Care. "Provision of Hospital Service and Quality of Care for Negroes," in its *Hospital Care in the United States,* pp. 163-67. New York: Commonwealth Fund, 1947.

Committee to End Discrimination in Chicago Medical Institutions. "What Color Are Your Germs?" *Journal of the National Medical Association* 47 (July 1955), 264-67.

Cornely, Paul B. "Segregation and Discrimination in Medical Care in the United States." *American Journal of Public Health* 46 (September 1956): 1074-81.

Cornely, Paul B. "Trend in Racial Integration in Hospitals in the United States." *Journal of the National Medical Association* 49 (January 1957): 8-10.

Cornely, Paul B. "Trends in Public Health Activities among Negroes in 96 Southern Counties During 1930-1939." *Journal of the National Medical Association* 34 (1942): 3-11.

"Court Finds Voluntary Hospital Subject to Fourteenth Amendment."
    Modern Hospital 102 (May 1964): 183.

Covington, Stuart. "The Case for the All-Negro Hospital." *Southern
    Hospitals* 19 (September 1951): 29-34.

Craig, John. "Black Hospitals": Their Prospects for Survival."
    Health Policy Research Group, School of Medicine,
    Georgetown University, Washington DC, 1978 (unpublished).

"The Crushing Irony of Deluxe Jim Crow." Editorial. *Journal of the
    National Medical* Association 44 (1952): 386-87.

Cunningham, Robert M., Jr. "Hospitalization for Negroes: Are
    Hospitals For the Sick - Or Just Some of the Sick?"
    Editorial. *Modern Hospital* 76 (June 1951): 51.

Dailey, U. G. "The New Hospital Era." *Journal of the National
    Medical Association* 22 (July/September 1930): 167-68.

Dailey, U. G. "The Negro in Medicine." *Journal of the National
    Medical Association* 34 (1942): 118-19.

Davis, Michael M. "What Color Is Health?" *Survey Graphic* 36
    (January 1947): 85-86.

Davis Michael M., and Smythe, Hugh H. "Providing Adequate
    Health Service to Negroes." *Journal of Negro Education* 18
    (1949): 305-17.

"The Dawn of a Better Day." *Journal of the National Medical
    Association* 17 (1925): 209-10.

Dent, Albert W. "Hospital Service and Facilities Available to
    Negroes in the United States." *Journal of Negro Education*
    18 (Summer 1949): 326-32.

"Detroit NAACP Opposes New Segregated Hospital." *Journal of the
    National Medical Association* 46 (1954): 68.

"Dingell Bill to Bar Discrimination under Hill-Burton Law." *Journal
    of the National Medical Association* 55 (1963): 185.

"Dingell Bill to End Hospital Discrimination Under the Hill-Burton
    Act." *Journal of the National Medical Association* 54 (1962):
    388-89.

Downing, L. C. "Early Negro hospitals." *Journal of the National
    Medical Association* 33 (1941): 13-18.

"Discrimination in North Carolina Hospitals." *Journal of the National Medical Association* 55 (January 1963): 57-58.

Dumas, A. W. "The Private Hospital." Editorial. *Journal of the National Medical Association* 25 (1933): 130-31.

Ewing, Oscar R. "The President's Health Program and The Negro." *Journal of Negro Education* 18 (1949): 436-43.

"Factors Influencing the Fate of the Negro Hospital." Editoral. *Journal of the National Medical Association* 59 (1967): 217-19.

"Federal Court Rules Bias in Federally Aided Hospitals Unconstitutional." *Journal of the National Medical Association* 55 (1963): 558.

"Fort Lauderdale, Florida, Hospital Controversy." *Journal of the National Medical Association* 52 (May 1960): 210.

Foster, J. T. "Survey: What's Ahead for Negro Hospitals?" *Modern Hospital* 109 (November 1967): 114-16.

"Fourth Imhotep National Conference on Hospital Integration." *Journal of the National Medical Association* 52 (1960): 283-85.

Freeman, Andrew A. "Hospital Integration in Columbus, Ohio." *Journal of the National Medical Association* 50 (July 1959): 301-302.

Friedman, Emily. "Private Black Hospitals: A Long Tradition Faces Change." *Hospitals* 55 (July 1, 1981): 65-68.

Gage, Nina D. "Hospital Facilities for Negro Patients in the South." *Bulletin of the American Hospital Association* 6 (July 1932): 126-28.

Garvin, Charles Herbert. "Post-War Planning for 'Negro' Hospitals." Editorial. *Journal of the National Medical Association* 37 (1945): 28-29.

Ghee, Euclid P. "A Plea to Admittance of Negro Doctors to Municipal Hospital Staffs," *Journal of the National Medical Association* 28 (August 1936): 102-105.

Givens, John T. "Access to a Hospital for Every Race Doctor." *Journal of the National Medical Association* 38 (1946): 35-36.

"Go and Build One for Yourselves." Editorial. *Journal of the National Medical Association* 26 (1934): 29-30.

Green, H. M. "A Brief Study of the Hospital Situation among Negroes." *Journal of the National Medical Association* 22 (1930): 112-14.

Green, H. M. "The Hospital Survey." *Journal of the National Medical Association* 21 (1929): 13-14.

Green, H. M. "Hospitals and Public Health Facilities for Negroes." *Proceedings of the National Conference of Social Work* 55 (1928): 178-80.

Green, H. M. *A More or Less Critical Review of the Hospital Situation among Negroes in the United States.* n.d., circa 1930.

"Greensboro, North Carolina, Group Files Historic Suit against Hospital Exclusion." *Journal of the National Medical Association* 54 (1962): 259.

Guzman, Jessie Parkhurst. "Negro Hospitals." In Jessie Parkhurst Guzman, *Negro Year Book: a Review of Events Affecting Negro Life, 1941-46.* Tuskegee Institute, Alabama: Department of Records and Research, Tuskegee Institute, 1947, pp. 336-38.

Guzman, Jessie Parkhurst, Jones, Lewis W., and Hall, Woodrow, eds. "Hospitals in 1952." In their *Negro Year Book: A Review of Events Affecting Negro Life.* New York: William H. Wise, 1952, pp. 166-68.

Hall, George C. "Negro Hospitals." *Southern Workman* 39 (October 1910): 551-54.

"H.E.W. Conference on Elimination of Hospital Discrimination." *Journal of the National Medical Association* 56 (September 1964): 445-46.

"Hill-Burton, 'Separate But Equal' Provision Unconstitutional." *Journal of the National Medical Association* 53 (1961): 647-48.

Hirsch, E. F. "The Hospital Care of Negroes and the Appointment of
    Negro Physicians to Medical Staffs of Hospitals in Chicago."
    Proceedings of the Institute of Medicine of Chicago 23
    (November 15, 1960): 156-59.
"History of the Imhotep National Conference on Hospital Integration."
    Journal of the National Medical Association 54 (January
    1962): 116-19.
Hornsby, John A. "Some Special Problems of Southern Hospitals."
    Tansactions of the American Hospital Association 32 (1930):
    638-45.
Horty, J. F. "Simkins Case Creates Civil Rights Pattern: Simkins vs.
    Moses H. Cone Memorial Hospital." *Modern Hospital* 102
    (June 1964): 40-44, 158.
"Hospital Discrimination and the Sixth Imhotep Conference."
    Editorial. *Journal of the National Medical Association* 54
    (1962): 253-55.
"Hospital Discrimination Must End!" Editorial. *Journal of the
    National Medical Association* 45 (July 1953): 284-86.
"Hospital Personnel Shortages." Editorial. *Journal of the National
    Medical Association* 42 (1950): 115-16.
"Hospital Provision for the Negro Race." *Journal of the American
    Medical Association* 94 (1930): 1414-1415.
"Hospital Survey." *Opportunity* 7 (1929): 145.
"Hospitals of the Black Community." *Urban Health* 1 (June 1972):
    20-23, 36.
"Hospitals and Civil Rights-A Special Report." *Modern Hospital* 101
    (July 1963): 21-22.
"Hospitals in Prospect." Editorial. *Journal of the National Medical
    Association* 14 (1922): 165.
"The Imhotep National Conference on Hospital Integration." *Journal
    of the National Medical Association* 49 (1957): 55-57.
"Implementation of the Civil Rights Act in Medical Areas: Federal
    Rules and Regulations." *Journal of the National Medical
    Association* 57 (1965): 157-63.
"Infirmary for Negroes, at Savannah, Geo." *Charleston Medical
    Journal and Review* 7 (1952): 724.

"Integration of Hospital Staffs and Medical Institutions in Louisville, Kentucky." *Journal of the National Medical Association* 52 (July 1960): 286-87.

"Integration Only Practicable Goal." Editorial. *Journal of the National Medical Association* 43 (1951): 340.

"Integration: What Is Hospital's Role?" *Hospitals* 37 (October 16, 1963): 17-21.

"Investigation of Negro Hospitals." *Journal of the American Medical Association* 92 (1929): 1375-1376.

Jack, Homer A. "Is Segregation Really Necessary?" *The Modern Hospital.* 76(6) (June 1951): 52-55.

Jackson, Algernon Brashear. "Hospitals and Health." *Journal of the National Medical Association* 22 (1930): 115-19.

Jackson, Algernon Brashear. "Public Health and the Negro." *Journal of the National Medical Association* 15 (1923): 256-59.

Jackson, E. A. "The Need of Better Hospital Facilities among Our People." *Journal of the National Medical Association* 13 (1921): 57-58.

Jason, Robert S. "Our Hospitals and the Negro: Keynote Address of Imhotep National Conference on Hospital Integration." *Journal of the National Medical Association* 50 (March 1958): 144-45.

"Javits Bill to End Hospital Discrimination under Hill Burton." *Journal of the National Medical Association* 54 (1962): 120-21.

"Javits Re-Introduces Hill Bill to Amend Hill-Burton Law." *Journal of the National Medical Association* 55 (1963): 345.

Javits, Jacob K. "Challenge Hospital Segregation." *Journal of the National Medical Association* 54 (July 1962): 504-505.

Johnson, Charles S., and Associates. "Health Facilities and Training." In Charles S. Johnson and Associates, *Into the Main Stream: A Survey of Best Practices in Race Relations in the South.* Chapel Hill: University of North Carolina Press, 1947, pp. 231-53.

Johnson, Everett A. "The Civil Rights Act of 1964-What It Means for Hospitals." *Hospitals* 38 (November 16, 1964): 51-54.

Johnson, J. L. "The Supply of Negro Health Personnel-Physicians."
    Journal of Negro Education 18 (1949): 346-56.

Jones, G. A. "A Survey to Determine the Extent of Hospital
    Discrimination in Pennsylvania: A Preliminary Report."
    Journal of the National Medical Association 56 (March
    1964): 206-207.

Julius Rosenwald Fund. *Negro Hospitals: A Compilation of Available
    Statistics.* Chicago: The Fund: 1931.

Kelly, William M. "The Romance of a Negro Sanitarium in Harlem."
    Opportunity. (June 1929): 177-78

Kenney, John A. "Report of Survey of Hospital Committee, Inter-
    Racial Committee of Montclair, New Jersey." *Journal of the
    National Medical Association* 23 (July/September): 97-109.

Kenney, John A. "The Hospital Idea Essentially Altruistic." *Journal
    of the National Medical Association* 4 (July-September 1912):
    193-99.

Kenney, John A. *The Negro in Medicine.* Tuskegee, Alabama:
    1912.

Kenney, John A. "The Negro's Position in Medicine." *Journal of the
    National Medical Association* 41 (1949): 31-33.

Kenney, John A. "Hospitals and Health Centers." Editorial. *Journal
    of the National Medical Association* 39 (1947): 38.

Kenney, John A. "The Interracial Committee of Montclair, New
    Jersey: Report of Survey of Hospital Committee." *Journal
    of the National Medical Association* 23 (1931): 97-109.

Kenney, John A. "The Negro Hospital Renaissance." *Journal of the
    National Medical Association* 22 (1930): 109-112.

Kenney, John A. "A Reasonable Program for Our Hospitalization
    Movement." *Journal of the National Medical Association* 23
    (1931): 158-60.

Kenney, John A. "A Plea for Interracial Cooperation." *Journal of
    the National Medical Association* 37 (1945): 121-24.

Langer, E. "Hospital Discrimination: HEW Criticized by Civil
    Rights Groups." *Science* 149 (September 17, 1965): 355-57.

Lattimore, J.A.C. "Address of the Outgoing President." *Journal of
    the National Medical Association* 40 (1948): 231-35.

"Lawsuit Charges Segregation under Hill-Burton Is Unconstitutional."
    Modern Hospital 98 (March 1962): 20.
Lee, Andre L. "Black Community Hospitals: A Quest for Survival."
    Urban Health 13 (March 1984): 46-47.
Manhattan Medical Society. *Equal Opportunity-No More-No Less!:
    An Open Letter to Mr. Edwin R. Embree, President of the
    Julius Rosenwald Fund.* New York, 28 January 1931.
Mann, Joseph B., Jr. "Black Community's Crisis of Care Hits
    Hospitals and Consumers." *Hospitals* 51 (March 16, 1977):
    70-73.
Marcinick, Edward. "Physicians, Hospitals, and the Negro Patient."
    Journal of the National Medical Association 50 (July 1963):
    346-49.
Maund, Alfred. *The Untouchables: The Meaning of Segregation in
    Hospitals.* New Orleans: Southern Conference Educational
    Fund, 1952.
McFall, T. Carr. "Needs for Hospital Facilities and Physicians in
    Thirteen Southern States." *Journal of the National Medical
    Association* 42 (1950): 235-56.
McNeil, Dorothy, and Williams, Robert. "Wide Range of Causes
    Found for Hospitals Closures." *Hospitals* 52 (December 1,
    1978): 76-81.
"Memphis NAACP Branch Rescinds Endorsement of Negro Hospital."
    Journal of the National Medical Association 44 (1952): 314-
    15.
"Merited Recognition." Editorial. *Modern Hospital* 57 (September
    1941): 50.
Merritt, Robert. "Black Hospitals." *Black Enterprise* 5 (February
    1975): 18-19.
Mille r, Joseph M. "Demise of Provident Hospital." Letter.
    Journal of the National Medical Association 78 (1986): 919-
    20.
Miller, W.H. "What Is Ours, We Should Conserve." *Journal of the
    National Medical Association* 24 (August 1932): 30-34.
"Milwaukee Hospital Integration Story." *Journal of the National
    Medical Association* 51 (July 1959): 300-301.

Minton, Russell F. "The Hospital as a Humanitarian Institution, with
    Special Reference To Negro Hospitals." *Journal of the
    National Medical Association* 39 (1947): 72-73.
Morris, John P. "The Denial of Staff Positions to Negro Physicians:
    A Violation of the Sherman Act." *Journal of the National
    Medical Association* 52 (1960): 211-15.
Mullner, Ross, Brye, Calvin S., and Kubal, Joseph D. "Five Year
    Trend Shows Urban Community Hospitals at Risk for
    Closure." *Urban Health* 11 (April 1982): 36-39.
Murray, Peter Marshall. "Hospital Provision for the Negro Race."
    Bulletin of the American Hospital Association 4 (1930): 37-
    46.
"NAACP 1961 Health Resolutions." *Journal of the National Medical
    Association* 53 (1961): 648-49.
"NAACP Request Raises Issue of No Negro Doctors on Hospital
    Medical Staff." *Modern Hospital* 93 (December 1959): 160.
"N.A.A.C.P. in Medicine: A Break-through Is Taking Place." Series
    of articles. *Modern Hospital* 79 (August 1952): 67-79, ff.
"National Conference on title VI-Civil Rights Act of 1964." *Journal
    of the National Medical Association* 57 (1965): 163-65.
National Medical Association. "Council on Medical Education and
    Hospitals." *Journal of the National Medical Association* 42
    (1950): 334-36.
National Urban League. *Report of the Hospital Committee.*
    Washington, 1963.
"The Need for Advanced Training Opportunities for Physicians and
    Dentists in Training Institutions." *Journal of the National
    Medical Association* 39 (1947): 237-40.
"Negro Doctors and Their Hospitals." Editorial. *Opportunity* 3
    (August 1925): 227.
"Negro Hospital Needs and How They Should Be Met." *Modern
    Hospital* 35 (September 1930): 86.
"Negro Hospitals Urged to Qualify for A.C.S. and Blue Cross
    Approval." *Modern Hospital* 62 (January 1944): 45.
"Negro Medical Center Planned at Provident Hospital, Chicago."
    National Negro Health News (January-March 1946): 3-4.

"Negroes in Medicine: A Break-Through Is Taking Place." *The Modern Hospital* 79 (2) (August 1952): 67-79, 140.

"New Epochal Federal Court Decision against Hospital Discrimination." *Journal of the National Medical Association* 56 (1964): 282-85.

"New Jersey Hospital Survey" *Journal of the National Medical Association* 42 (May 1950): 183-84.

"Of Hospitals, Doctors, and the Constitution." *Hospitals* 38 (June 1, 1964): 116-17.

"The Old Order Changeth." Editorial. *Journal of the National Medical Association* 46 (1954): 65-67.

Olordson, Arsenio, Jr., "Poor Lose Access to Care as Community Hospitals Close." *The Chicago Reporter* 17 (5) (May 1988): 3-5.

"On the Firing Line." Editorial. *Journal of the National Medical Association* 23 (1931): 92-93.

"Our Hospital Problems." Editorial. *Journal of the National Medical Association* 21 (1929): 114-16.

Oppenheimer, H. C. "Non-Discriminatory Hospital Service." *Mental Hygiene* 24 (April 1945): 47-52.

Parker, M. L. "Civil Rights Act of 1964." *Health, Education, and Welfare Indicators* 8 (August 1964): v-xviii.

Payne, Larah D. "Survival of Black Hospitals in the U.S. Health Care System: A Case Study." Lennox S. Yearwood (ed.), *Black Organizations: Issues on Survival Techniques*. Lanham, MD: University Press of America, Inc., 1980, pp. 205-11.

Peniston, Reginald. "A Racial View of Medical Education." *Journal of the National Medical Association* 79 (1987): 143-45.

Perkins, Theodore. "The Case of the Negro Administrator." *Modern Hospital* 76 (June 1951): 61-63.

Phillips, Donald F. "Small Urban Hospital-A Question of Survival." *Hospitals* 48 (October 1, 1974): 71-74.

Phillips, George M. "The Public Mental Hospital: An Example of Minority Isolation." *Journal of the National Medical Association* 57 (January 1965): 47-52.

Pinkney, Deborah.   "Future Looks Bleak for Black Hospitals."
     American Medical News, 10 April 1987, pp. 1, 50.
"A Plea for More Hospitals for Negroes."   *Modern Hospital* 25
     (1925): 126.
Ponton, T. R.   "Hospital Service for Negroes."   *Hospital Management*
     51 (March 1941): 14-15, 50.
Postell, William Dosite.   "Slave Hospitals."   In William Dosite
     Postell, *The Health of Slaves on Southern Plantations*, pp.
     129-41. 1951. Reprint. Gloucester, MA: Peter Smith,
     1970.
"Present Status of the Negro Physician and Negro Patient." *Journal*
     of the National Medical Association 37 (1935): 79-80.
Pringle, Henry T., and Pringle, Katharine. *The Color in Medicine*.
     New York: Committee of 100. Reprinted from *Saturday*
     Evening Post, 24 January 1948.
"Problems of Black Hospital Administrators." *Urban Health* 6 (April
     1977): 42-43, 47-50.
"Proceedings of the Imhotep National Conference on Hospital
     Integration." *Journal of the National Medical Association* 49
     (1957): 189-201, 272-73, 352-56, 50; (1958): 66-76, 142-
     44, 224-33.
"Proceedings of the Seventh Imhotep National Conference on Hospital
     Integration." *Journal of the National Medical Association* 55
     (1963): 329-43.
"Proceedings of the Sixth Imhotep Conference." *Journal of the*
     National Medical Association 54 (1962): 499-507.
Procope, John L.   "The Colored Man and the Blue Cross." *Modern*
     Hospital 62 (April 1944): 59.
"Professional and Public Focus on Hospital Discrimination," *Journal*
     of the National Medical Association 55 (January 1964): 95-
     96.
"Proposed Agenda: Council on Medical Education and Hospitals.
     National Medical Association." *Journal of the National*
     Medical Association 41 (1949): 185-86.

"Proposal for Separate Negro Hospital in St. Petersburg, Florida, Protested." *Journal of the National Medical Association* 52 (1960): 216.

"Public Works Administration." *Journal of the National Medical Association* 29 (1937): 71.

"Racial Barriers Are Breaking Down." *Modern Hospital* 82 (April 1954): 77-80.

"A Recommended Hospital Program." Editorial. *Journal of the National Medical Association* 23 (1931): 140-43.

"Reference List of Titles in This Journal, 1950-1956, Relating to Anti-Discrimination Developments in Medicine." *Journal of the National Medical Association* 49 (1957): 58-61.

Reitzes, Dietrich C., and Reitzes, H. "Factors Which Block or Facilitate Integration in the Field of Medicine." *Interracial Review* (September 1960): 180-87.

"Resolution on Hospital Discrimination." *Journal of the National Medical Association* 45 (1953): 444.

"Resolutions in Health Area of the 1952 Annual Convention of the NAACP." *Journal of the National Medical Association* 44 (1952): 466.

Reynolds, Clyde L. "The Fiscal Results of Segregation." *Modern Hospital* 76 (June 1951): 64.

Rice, Don A. "The Application of Multi-Hospital Arrangements to Black Urban Institutions: Opportunities for Survival and Growth." Paper presented at the meeting of the Black Caucus of Health Workers of the American Public Health Association, Detroit, Michigan, October 1980.

Richings, G. F. "Hospitals and Homes." In G. F. Richings, *Evidences of Progress among Colored People*, pp. 380-98. Philadelphia: George S. Ferguson, 1896.

Richings, G. F. "Hospitals and Homes." In G. F. Richings, *Evidences of Progress among Colored People*, pp. 392-410. Philadelphia: George S. Ferguson, 1905.

Ridgway, Frances. "Atlanta Opinions Clash over Role of the Negro Hospital." *Modern Hospital* 109 (November 1967): 118-20.

Robinson, E. I. "President's Annual Address." *Journal of the National Medical Association* 38 (1946): 210-12.

Roman, C. V. "Our Hospitals." *Journal of the National Medical Association* 22 (1930): 167.

Rorem, C. Rufus. "'No Color Line' But 'No Alternative.'" *Modern Hospital* 76 (June 1951): 57.

Ross, Mary. "Improved Negro Hospital Facilities Is Hopeful Sign for the South." *Modern Hospital* 39 (October 1932): 53-60.

Royal, Frank S. "Survival of Black Health Care Providers." *Journal of the National Medical Association* 73 (1981): 915-16.

Roylance, Frank D. "Black Hospitals in Critical Condition." *The Evening Sun* (Baltimore). September 23-26, 1985.

Sager, Alan. "Urban Hospital Closings in the Face of Racial Change." *Health Law Project Library Bulletin* 5 (June 1980): 169-81.

Sampson, Calvin C. "Death of the Black Community Hospital: Fact or Fiction." Editorial. *Journal of the National Medical Association* 66 (1974): 165.

Scheele, Leonard A. "The Health Status and Health Education of Negroes-A General Introductory Statement." *Journal of Negro Education* 18 (1949): 200-208.

Schleifer, C. "Desegregation of a State Mental Hospital for Negroes: A Study of Staff Attitudes." *American Journal of Psychology* 121 (April 1965): 947-52.

"Second Imhotep National Conference on Hospital Integration." *Journal of the National Medical Association* 50 (1958): 381-83.

"Second Suit Filed against Wilmington, North Carolina, Hospital." *Journal of the National Medical Association* 53 (1961): 531.

Seham, Max J. "Discrimination against the Negro in Medicine: A Paradox in the Democracy-Battlefront on Integration." *Journal of the National Medical Association* 56 (March 1964): 155-59.

Seham, Max J. "Discrimination against the Negro in Hospitals." *New England Journal of Medicine* 271 (October 29, 1964): 940-43.

Shah, N. D., and McGhee, N. "Shift from Predominantly White to Predominantly Black Staff: A Retrospective Study Relating to Surgical Care." *Journal of the National Medical Association* 7 (1980): 677-81.

"Should Negroes Accept Jim Crow Hospitals." *Negro Digest* (March 1946): 72-77.

"Southern Hospital Facilities for Negroes." *Survey* 88 (1952): 178-79.

Smith, S. W. "Deficiency of Bed Space and Suggestions for Remedies." *Journal of the National Medical Association* 33 (1941): 26-29.

Stritch, Samuel Cardinal. "Interracial Justice in Hospitals." *Journal of the National Medical Association* 48 (March 1956): 133-34.

Stubbs, Frederick D. "The Purpose of the Community Hospital." *Journal of the National Medical Association* 36 (1944): 152-54.

Synder, J. D. "Race Bias in Hospitals: What the Civil Rights Commission Found." *Hospital Management* 96 (November 1963): 52-54.

Taylor, Holman. "Cooperation Between the Races in the Practice of Medicine." *Journal of the National Medical Association* 33 (1941): 8-13.

"Text of H.E.W. Order on Nondiscrimination by Hill-Burton Applicants." *Journal of the National Medical Association* 56 (1964): 349.

"There Is Still a Mission Field at Home." Editorial. *Hospital Progress* 34 (November 1953): 45-46.

"Third Imhotep National Conference on Hospital Integration." *Journal of the National Medical Association* 51 (1959): 299-303.

"Title VI and Hospitals." *Journal of the National Medical Association* 58 (1966): 212-13.

"Two Greensboro, N.C., Hospitals to Ask U.S. Supreme Court to Review Decision Barring 'Separate-But-Equal' Facilities." *Hospitals* 38 (16 January 1964): 19.

"Unanimous Appeals Court Decision Ends Bar on Negroes in North
     Carolina Hospital." *Hospitals* 38 (May 1, 1964): 86.

U.S. Commission on Civil Rights. *Equal Opportunity in Hospitals
     and Health Facilities: Civil Rights Policies under the Hill-
     Burton Program* (Washington, DC: U.S. Commission on
     Civil Rights, 1965).

United States Commission on Civil Rights. *Title VI ... One Year
     After: A Survey of Desegregation of Health and Welfare
     Services in the South.* (Washington, DC: Government
     Printing Office, 1966.)

United States Department of the Interior. Bureau of Education.
     "Hospitals and Nurse Training Schools." In *Negro
     Education*, vol. 1, p. 176. Washington: Government
     Printing Office, 1917.

Wesley, Nathaniel, Jr.   "Black Hospitals Listing and Selected
     Commentary: Searching for Survival." Washington, DC,
     1983. (Unpublished).

Wesley, Nathaniel, Jr.   "Dilemma of Black Community Hospitals."
     Urban Health 13 (November 1984): 38-39.

Wesley, Nathaniel, Jr.   "1986 Black Hospitals Listing and Selected
     Commentary: Tradition, Competition, and The Management
     of Change." Washington, DC, 1986. (Unpublished).

Williams, Edward B., Jr.   "A Negro Hospital Faces Change."
     Editorial. *Journal of the National Medical Association* 53
     (1961): 643-45.

"Wilmington, North Carolina, Physicians Sue for Hospital Privileges."
     Journal of the National Medical Association 48 (1956): 201-
     202.

Winston, M. E.   "Discussion. Some Special Problems of Southern
     Hospitals."   *Transactions of the American Hospital
     Association* 32 (1930): 648-52.

Work, Monroe N., ed.   "Hospitals and Nurse Training Schools."   In
     *Negro Year Book: An Annual Encyclopedia of the Negro,
     1921-1922*, pp. 370-72. Tuskegee Institute, Alabama: The
     Negro Year Book Publishing Co., 1922.

Work, Monroe N., ed. "Hospitals and Nurse Training Schools." In
    *Negro Year Book: An Annual Encyclopedia of the Negro,
    1925-1926*, pp. 416-20. Tuskegee Institute, Alabama: The
    Negro Year Book Publishing Co., 1926.
Work, Monroe, N., ed. "Hospitals and Nurse Training Schools." In
    *Negro Year Book: An Annual Encyclopedia of the Negro,
    1931-1932*, pp. 527-28. Tuskegee Institute, Alabama: The
    Negro Year Book Publishing Co., 1931.
Work, Monroe, N., ed. "Hospitals and Nurse Training Schools." In
    *Negro Year Book: An Annual Encyclopedia of the Negro,
    1937-1938*, pp. 290-92. Tuskegee Institute, Alabama: The
    Negro Year Book Publishing Co., 1937.
Younge, Walter A. "The President's Annual Address." *Journal of
    the National Medical Association* 39 (1947): 233-36.

Index

About the Authors

MITCHELL F. RICE is Professor of Political Science and Public Administration at Louisiana State University.

WOODROW JONES, JR. is Professor of Political Science at Texas A&M University. Together they edited *Contemporary Public Policy Perspectives and Black Americans* (Greenwood, 1984), in addition to other works.